MULTI-IMAGE MEDIA

The Instructional Media Library

Volume Number 9

MULTI-IMAGE MEDIA

Robert V. Bullough, Sr.
Educational Systems and Learning Resources
University of Utah

James E. Duane
Series Editor

Educational Technology Publications
Englewood Cliffs, New Jersey 07632

Library of Congress Cataloging in Publication Data

Bullough, Robert V
    Multi-image media.

    (The Instructional media library ; v. no. 9)
    Bibliography: p.
    1. Audio-visual materials. 2. Projectors.
I. Title. II. Series: Instructional media library ;
v. no. 9.
LB1043.B83   371.3'35   80-21341
ISBN 0-87778-169-9

Printed in the United States of America.

Library of Congress Catalog Card Number:
80-21341

International Standard Book Number:
0-87778-169-9

First Printing: January, 1981.

Table of Contents

MULTI-IMAGE MEDIA

1.

Introduction

The term "multi-image" has been defined in a number of different ways, none of which appears to be entirely adequate. The art of multi-image has evolved to the point where any attempt to come up with a succinct, dictionary-type description of it is quite difficult, if not impossible. Nevertheless, there are specific attributes that tend to characterize the medium. For example, the multi-image presentation is programmed in some manner. It is the programmer that makes everything work together, that permits the complicated sequencing to take place. Another characteristic is the tendency for producers to use three screens (although other combinations are to be found). Three screens seem to represent the optimal number for the average producer. They provide ample screen space without being overly cumbersome. Also, the lateral projection area represented by this screen combination comes very close to representing the visual angle—or the area that the eye covers—of the average viewer.

Additionally, sound is a very important part of most multi-image presentations. Although many filmstrips and some slide programs have printed captions that are integral to the visual frames, and other such media incorporate scripts which the presenter reads to the audience, such techniques are incompatible with the multi-image approach for the most

3

part. In multi-image, the audio is an integral and inseparable component of the total mix, an aspect of the overall experience without which much of the impact would be lost.

Other characteristics of the medium can be identified, but those listed above are the most definitive.

In the early days of multi-image, many of the pioneers found themselves dashing from one projector to another, manually pressing advance buttons to change the visuals, or to shut the projectors off and turn them on. At times, they would insert images and special effects using an overhead projector with transparencies, polarized spinners, and even dishes filled with various liquid dyes, which formed flowing patterns on the screen as the fluid was agitated and stirred about. The motion picture became part of the mix, and live talent sometimes put in an appearance.

Sometimes, entire teams of operators were involved in such shows. They would rehearse for hours on end in an effort to insure that a mistake-free presentation would result, but mistakes still seemed to creep in—human error was the culprit.

Today, the story is different. Given the proper equipment, the total presentation can be completely programmed, thereby relieving the operator of the anxiety and trauma that are connected with the hands-on approach. All this has been made possible by those ingenious devices known as programmers. Early programmers were rather simple when judged against current models. They were activated by pulses that were encoded onto one of the tracks of a stereo tape—the other track was used for the narration and related audio effects.

Recent innovations in miniaturization have resulted in the creation of subsequent generations of programmers that include those with electronic memory banks and models that are built around the microprocessor.

In reality, much of the newer hardware is far too expensive

to constitute a viable option for most schools. It will, in all probability, be necessary for the teacher who wishes to explore the medium to revert back to the "good old days" of manual button pressing. Or, it is sometimes possible to locate used, older model programmers that are in good condition and can be purchased for a modest sum. Also, brand-new programmers that use tone-generated signals are now being marketed for about $400.00 to $500.00 each. Such devices are quite functional, easy to use, and sturdy.

Although considered by many to be an art of very recent derivation, multi-image actually dates back to the year 1896, when a Frenchman, Claude Autant-Lara, used a series of screens of different formats to present a program on gold exploration. More recently, striking presentations utilizing innovative approaches have been created by Eastman Kodak Company, Walt Disney, and producers in many foreign countries (notably Germany).

The educator is surely justified in asking how multi-image can be applied to the field of education. This publication will address this concern. It will describe methods and techniques that will enable the interested teacher to create and present his or her own multi-image presentations.

2.

Objectives

Although this book is not programmed and is not structured around behavioral objectives, nevertheless it seems advisable and worthwhile to identify a number of competencies that can be attained through its use. It is difficult to specify such competencies in a manner that is all-inclusive, for it is hoped that information gleaned from this publication will serve to initiate further research into yet more challenging types of endeavors with the multi-image medium. Therefore, the following list must be considered as a somewhat provisional one, subject to modification on the basis of the reader's needs, interests, and motivation.

After having worked through this book, you should be able to:

1. Define the term "multi-image."
2. List advantages and disadvantages claimed for the medium.
3. Describe three types of behaviors, and indicate how multi-image can be used as an instructional medium in each of these.
4. List at least five special techniques that are more or less unique to multi-image.
5. Describe a logical sequence that might be used in planning a multi-image presentation.
6. Describe ways in which titles and graphics can be

created. Tell how the resulting visuals can be converted to the slide format.

7. List several techniques that can be used to create special effects in slides.

8. Describe a light box or table, tell how it would be used. Describe the process of traying slides.

9. Tell how you can mix sound from several sources onto a single tape. Tell what a "music" library is.

10. Tell what a programmer is; describe in general terms how it works. Describe in general terms how you would program a multi-image presentation.

11. Describe how you would prepare a room for a multi-image presentation.

12. List the kinds of equipment that would be used in a typical multi-image presentation. In general terms, describe the equipment.

13. Describe several ways that you might utilize multi-image in the classroom or similar situation; or, better still, actually utilize the medium.

14. Involve students in projects that are based on this approach; or, describe in detail several projects that could be used with students or others.

15. Locate terms in the Glossary; locate sources for equipment and materials in the appropriate chapters of this book.

3.

Multi-Image
as a Communication Medium

Arguments have been presented in favor of the multi-image approach to instruction as well as against it. Those who hold to the concept of a single-channel perceptual system use as the major defense of their position the idea of "channel overload." On the other hand, those who favor multi-image can present some rather convincing data to support their point of view. Let us first consider some of the positive attributes that are claimed for multi-image; then, we shall examine some of the arguments put forth by its detractors.

In her book *Philosophy in a New Key*, Susanne Langer discusses the concept of "non-discursive symbolism," which involves the parallel processing of information. Put another way, objects and events that are perceived visually tend to enter the perceptual system and be processed simultaneously. On the other hand, verbal information, both spoken and written, is processed sequentially; that is, it enters the perceptual system as elements in a chain, which, when finally combined, represent the total thought. Language is, therefore, a "discursive" system.

The traditional manner in which the projected media (such as slide presentations and motion pictures) have been utilized is in a discursive sense, so to speak. That is, the slides are presented sequentially, one at a time, in order to build up to a cumulative idea. It must be recognized that events in the real world occur in just such a manner; however, they occur in a richly visual context—a context in which a wealth of pertinent information impinges simultaneously to become part of the event. Not so with the sequenced slide or motion picture presentation. In this case, the selected visuals are seen in their sterile black environment, existing as entities in a void. This comment is not made in a derogatory sense; it is meant, rather, as a comment on the differences between the media under discussion.

The utilization of multi-image tends to overcome, to some extent, the problem described above. The use of simultaneous images in a well-planned presentation permits the students to synthesize their own montages, just as they would do in real life—selecting here and discarding there, emphasizing this aspect of the display while de-emphasizing some other aspect. Teachers find the multi-image presentation to be useful where comparisons are to be made among and between various items. Unless a slide contains multiple images (which it seldom does), comparisons must be made in a sequential manner, comparing the content of one slide with that of the next one, and so on—the feature of simultaneity is lacking in such an approach.

Comparisons can be of many kinds. For example, the objective might be that the individual will be able to distinguish a bird of prey from those birds that do not belong to this group. The multi-image, large screen arrangement permits instances of both types of birds to be simultaneously loaded into the image area. This is a rather low-level kind of use for the medium, but it does illustrate one application. At a different level, comparisons can be made of stages in a process—the stages being displayed simultaneously, or, perhaps better still, sequentially from the initial to the last image, with the final display showing all stages at the same time.

Another advantage that is claimed for the multi-image approach is that it more closely approximates the real world of objects and events than does the single screen approach. As we look around, we are aware that the environment surrounds us. Even though our peripheral vision is hazy, and it becomes increasingly more so as the visual field extends away from us, we are still cognizant of the fact that *something* is there. The wide screen, multi-image approach, when properly designed and utilized, comes close to approximating this effect.

Where resources are available, screens have been arranged in such a manner that they extend in a 360° circle to enfold the audience completely. Such arrangements have been used by business, and at professional conventions such as those held annually by the Association for Educational Communications and Technology. Disney installed such a facility at Anaheim in the early 70's, and other instances can be mentioned. Such expensive installations may well be out of reach for the typical public school; however, a few innovative teachers and students have experimented with suspended bed sheets which serve as rear-view screens upon which various projectors stationed at points around the room project their images.

At any rate, merely extending a screen straight across a wall expands the image area to the point where the sense of a limitless visual field is suggested. This gives a much more "real" effect than does the typical single screen approach. The single screen image is equivalent to the effect that results when a person looks at a picture in a book, or, when the view is through a door or a window from within a darkened room. The visual display is effectively framed and becomes but a section of the potentially available field.

Additionally, the multi-image approach can make possible the presentation of a greater amount of information in a given time-span. But, this seems to be the area in which most criticism of the medium arises. There are certain precautions that can be taken to prevent the problem of "overload" from arising. For one, it is necessary that the visuals, and the verbal material, not compete among themselves. All inputs must be relevant; otherwise, confusion can result and interpretation will suffer. We might use as an example of relevance a marching band. Imagine yourself standing on the curb as the band goes by. You are bombarded with a multiplicity of sights and sounds—the drummer and the sounds he makes, the drum major and the majorettes, the blaring horns, the brightly-colored flags, and so forth. In one sense, the effect is one of sequence, a characteristic of language and of tradition-al slide shows. But, look again—is it not a simultaneous display that confronts you? Glance down the line and you can take in the entire event at one time—not the details, but the overall "feel" of it. Now, be selective. Let your eye rove here and there, and let your ears be selective also. Note that regardless of where your attention is directed, everything is relevant to the concept of "marching band." All of the various inputs add up to an experience of the total event that is much more rich and accurate than would be the case if you were watching the band move by from a position behind a knot hole in a fence—a situation that would cause the effect to be more nearly like that of the sequential nature of the more traditional presentation modes.

Given the simultaneous impact of a multitude of images that is afforded by the multi-image approach, the task of the viewer is rather different from that required when the single screen approach is used. The viewer has greater latitude to select from the available data and to create a vignette that is uniquely his or her own. The objective is not that the viewer decode ALL of the information presented (an impossible task at best), but that from the assembled, selected bits and pieces he or she come up with a result that has a reasonable correspondence with the aims of the individual who is utilizing the medium.

One final advantage for the multi-image approach can be

mentioned—it can be sensational, spectacular, overwhelming. In some instances, the imparting of specific information may not be the principal objective, or it may not be a consideration at all. Perhaps the reason for using the medium is to generate an emotional atmosphere or to create a particular environment. In cases such as this, the retention of factual information is secondary to the affective experience that the observer undergoes. The teacher might ask, "How does such an approach tie in with educational objectives?" Certainly, if our objectives are strictly related to the acquisition of factual material, there may well be no legitimate reason to use an approach such as that described. However, if we believe that education should extend beyond mere rote learning, then the value of such emotion-based approaches becomes obvious—if carefully designed, presentations of this nature can affect attitudes, lead to the development of vivid impressions, and stimulate the creative potential of students.

On the other hand, this exciting, emotion-charged aspect of multi-image can be, and generally is, present even though the major objective is to teach specific concepts or principles. Obviously, the pacing must be modified, and the amount of visual and verbal information that is loaded into the presentation must be carefully controlled. It is at this point that the value of multi-image begins to decline.

In summary, the advantages that are claimed for the multi-image approach are:

1. This approach more nearly duplicates the way in which stimuli are presented to our perceptual system in the real world. Or, it might be better to say that the world consists of a vast array of simultaneously existing objects and events with which our active perceptual system deals in a selective fashion.

2. The wide-screen format is a more natural way of displaying visual material than is the single or small screen format. We are surrounded by our environment; it does not exist as a series of framed instances.

3. More information can be presented in a given time-span with the multi-image approach; consequently, this method is more efficient than is the traditional technique.

4. The multi-image approach can be sensational and attention getting.

In contradiction to the arguments that the attributes of multi-image are positive are those that suggest that the simultaneous presentation of masses of information leads to confusion and "overload." This can be the case, but through careful design such problems can be prevented from creeping in. Nevertheless, it will be of interest to examine the supposed mechanism that serves as the basis for much of the criticism directed at the simultaneous presentation of large amounts of information in different modes.

Broadbent developed a model of the perceptual system that was based on the concept of a single-channel that permitted only so much information to pass through it in a given period of time. An oversimplified example of how such a system works is illustrated by an irrigation ditch that has a single pipe through which the water passes to reach a particular plot. During those times when there is an over-abundance of water in the ditch, the pipe fills up and, once full, can pass no additional water. Several pipes running from the ditch solve the problem by providing the over-supply with additional routes. This illustrates the multiple-channel concept. Broadbent's experiments were conducted with sound, and the ears were thought of as channels—one for each ear. You can see how such an experiment might be controlled, with simultaneous but different sounds entering the two ears. It is a bit difficult to use this same approach when vision is involved. However, there are ways in which a kind of "overload" can be achieved experimentally. Additionally, the audio and the visual can be intermixed, thus resulting in a combination that approximates an actual multi-image presentation.

The findings derived from studies that have involved the simultaneous presentation of multiple inputs show that, under certain conditions, a kind of "overloading" can result. That is to say, comprehension is less than that which is obtained through the use of linear presentations. Findings of this nature tend to support the contention that multi-image presentations can, in effect, "overload" the perceptual system. Such conclusions should be accepted with caution. For one thing, the research is relatively sparse; additionally, only under certain conditions and constraints do such results occur.

A number of design strategies can be implemented that, used singly or in different combinations, will successfully prevent or diminish the overload problem (at least a large part of it). As mentioned earlier, relevance is of great importance. The various visuals and verbals should have a relationship with one another. Also, simplicity is an important factor, not only in the content but also in the design of the material as well. Another factor is pacing. It has been determined that the eye actively scans a picture, coming to rest on, or fixating, those points that are of greatest interest. The eye scans and fixates at a pace that has definite limitations. In other words, if the visuals are so information-laden that the eye cannot derive from them the essential content in the time-span allowed, then information will be lost.

The nature of the audience must be considered also as should, quite obviously, the objectives of the lesson or presentation. As previously mentioned, it may be more important to derive from a presentation the gross "meaning" rather than the microscopic "facts." If such is the primary objective, information density can be quite high, and the consideration of channel overload becomes rather unimportant.

In instances where specific facts are to be learned, the

problem of overload can be addressed through such strategies as substantially slowing the pacing, and using visuals and verbals that provide relevant cues. Studies that relate to visual recall—that is, the ability to remember pictures and details in pictures—indicate that in order for the observer to remember certain details of a visual, he or she must have sufficient time to fixate on those details. That is to say, his or her eyes must actually come to rest, even for the briefest moment, on the relevant details. Obviously, we cannot remember what we do not see.

Where relevant cues are concerned, research has shown that information that is not relevant tends to interfere with our ability to remember the relevant details; and, conversely, in situations where the information is highly relevant, greater increments of learning accrue. To illustrate this in a more concrete manner, the presentation of pictures and audio that contain cues that tend to be related will lead to increased learning, whereas presentations that include visuals and audio that contain unrelated cues will result in less than optimal learning. This sounds like just plain common sense, but it is reassuring to know that it has been proven experimentally. So, if we want our presentations to be as effective as possible, we can't use just any sound track that is handy as part of the program—it must be appropriate to the visuals. And the opposite is also true; visuals must be selected that are appropriate companions to a narration or musical selection. The visuals must be selected so that each one supports all of the others, and all of them taken together add up to the total effect that we desire.

4.

Utilization of Multi-Image

Although used in a number of settings with different audiences and varying goals, it appears that at this point in time the predominant reason for employing the multi-image medium in most schools is one that relates to its ability to attract attention and to stir the emotions. Educational objectives obviously extend beyond this level. If this were the primary application in learning institutions, it would be difficult to justify the time, cost, and effort that is involved in putting a presentation together.

Where educational applications are concerned, objectives can be established that extend from the emotional level through a continuum that includes the learning of specifics, such as factual material, at the opposite end. Multi-image has applications through the total continuum.

In actuality, we are just a bit ahead of ourselves. Here we are talking about the multi-image approach as if the selection of same were a foregone conclusion. We should back up and consider some of those things that are precursors to the selection of a given medium that serves as the major instructional component.

We should think in terms of what it is that we want to accomplish before considering the media. Then, we must survey the capabilities of the various media before we settle on a specific kind—at this point, we might very well select multi-image; but, then again, perhaps not.

Identifying the type of behavior that is to be taught is a useful first step in determining the media to be used. Behaviors can be categorized as cognitive, affective, and psychomotor. Cognitive behavior involves the recall of knowledge and the learning and application of intellectual skills. Affective behavior has to do with emotional behavior. It includes value-oriented activities, attitudes, and feelings. Psychomotor behavior requires coordinated muscular activity. It has to do with the physical manipulation of things, body movements, etc.

Cognitive behaviors may be broken down into three categories; these identify what the students do as a consequence of the instruction that they have received. The categories are (1) discriminated recall, (2) the use of rules, and (3) the classification of objects and events. Discriminated recall has to do with remembering factual data. When you remember your Social Security number or a friend's telephone number, you are practicing discriminated recall. More typically, educational applications involve the memorization of tables of numbers, names of people who are deemed important, symbols of various kinds, etc. The use of rules involves the application of a prescribed sequence of steps. When figuring the area of a circle or creating a flowchart, rules are used. Classification skills are closely related to concept development. In order to have a concept, a person must be able to properly classify instances of that concept. For example, in order to have the concept of formal balance, a person would have to correctly identify this quality, or the lack of it, in a variety of paintings, pictures, photographs, etc. A simple example of classification is when a student places his or her school subjects in "like" and "don't like" categories.

Now that we have looked at cognitive behaviors, let us consider the potential, or lack of same, for using multi-image as a medium for instruction. Discriminated recall is fostered through the use of strategies that provide for individualized learning and much rehearsal. This type of learning frequently takes place during the student's own time and at a place of his or her own choosing. Rules vary as to type; some involve the use of formulas, others involve simple step-by-step applications, while still others involve complex procedures (like landing an airplane). Depending on the nature of the rule, different strategies are used. Rules that involve computation require that arrangements be made to provide the students with ample time and sufficient assistance to enable them to perform adequately. Complex rules that involve special types of equipment can best be taught if the equipment is immediately available to the students.

When classifying objects and events, a wide array of instances should be provided. Depending upon the nature of the items being classified, various materials can be used for this purpose. When practicable, the actual objects might be employed; otherwise, media are useful here.

In an effort to determine the effectiveness of multi-image in the teaching of cognitive skills, researchers are conducting studies that involve the recall of factual information presented via this medium. Interestingly, the studies that have been conducted to date indicate that this is an effective way in which to present factual information. Indeed, the learning that accrued often is greater with multi-image than was the case when more traditional instructional methods were used. It should be noted that the studies are few in number and highly specific, and the findings cannot be widely generalized to school populations at this point in time. Nevertheless, this line of research may well lead to the formulation of design principles that can be used by the multi-image producer to insure that cognitive objectives, among others, can be realized with a high degree of certainty.

For more complex materials, it can be assumed that the multi-image medium has a rather limited application. This medium might be used, for example, to present comparisons when classification skills are being stressed. It might also be used if the thing to be recalled is highly visual in nature—in this instance, the presentation would require that a multitude of relevant cues be built into it. It should be mentioned that there are notable instances in which complex concepts that have no simple visual referents have been dealt with through the use of visual media. One example is the photo series on the Depression years that was produced by the Farm Security Administration. Although not in the multi-image format, these powerful photographs could well serve as the basis for such a presentation. Although the pictures do not get at the basic cause of the Depression, they build a powerful montage of the results. Attendant verbal information might well be used to enhance and enlarge on the concept.

On the other hand, if we subscribe to the idea that the least expensive strategy that is still effective should be used in instruction, then the limited application of multi-image to the teaching of cognitive skills will make its use untenable.

There are times when the multi-image presentation is used to give an overview or introduction to a predominantly cognitively-oriented unit. This is, in fact, the way in which the medium is typically tied in with the cognitive area. One instance that comes to mind is the introductory presentation for a university-level class on perception. The presentation includes some terminology, but it is basically a comparative visual overview of some selected theories of perception along with a look at how the human perceptual system works. Subsequent class sessions use more traditional methods to deal with specifics that are alluded to in the introductory unit. Considerable interest and curiosity are generated through the use of the initial multi-image presentation.

Let us now turn to the second area, that of affective behaviors. It is within this area that multi-image enjoys its greatest application and success. Most of the evidence supporting the effectiveness of the medium in this behavior area is based on assumptions. That is, conclusions are drawn on the basis of how people appear to react to a given presentation. However, in recent years a number of scientific studies has been conducted in an effort to prove statistically what we have generally tended to accept as being true because it *appeared* to be so. In controlled studies that compared multi-image to the single-image format, the former medium was found to be superior to the latter where affective behaviors were concerned. Although more research is needed in order to identify the specific attributes that foster increased affective responding, it is reassuring to know that the available data support the contention that multi-image is a powerful tool for the development of affective behaviors.

Multi-image is becoming increasingly popular as a medium to introduce tourists to a particular area. A number of cities, including Chicago and New Orleans, have elaborate presentations that are highly successful in motivating visitors to want to see more of the area. Of course, these programs also contain a cognitive element—anyone viewing them will come away with a store of new knowledge—but the emotional orientation generally predominates.

Many other uses that relate to the affective domain can be given, but we must finally ask the question: "How does all this fit into the realm of education?" One application that has been alluded to in a previous section is the use of the medium as an inspirational introduction to an instructional unit. When this is the primary application, the effort is directed toward creating an interest in the cognitive materials that will follow. This doesn't imply that dull materials will be made interesting through the use of a good introductory segment. It is to suggest that a heightened anticipation will lead to greater amounts of learning, if subsequent lessons are of such a nature that they build on the initial impetus provided.

A greater awareness of the importance of affective behaviors has led to the quest for ways to encourage their development. Multi-image has become the darling of many who are striving to address the problem of how best to deal with the teaching of content that is affectively oriented. Schools typically stress the teaching of things that have a strong cognitive flavor, for a number of reasons, among which is the relative ease with which these can be recognized, measured, and quantified. Affective behaviors are considerably more difficult to deal with; often, they are never externalized through observable behavior, and thus they are terribly difficult to measure. Additionally, the writing of objectives in this area is a formidable task, to say the least.

Nevertheless, there are certain rules-of-thumb that can be most helpful to the teacher as he or she attempts to assess the affective impact of a multi-image presentation. For example, attending behaviors can be observed. Check to see if the presentation appears to hold the attention of the group. It is fairly safe to conclude that such is the case if the audience seems caught up in the show—"plugged-in" to what is going on. Is there discussion following the presentation? This is a sure indication that interest was stimulated. However, without a more formal effort to determine what the discussion is about, we cannot safely conclude that it relates to the specific objectives around which the presentation was constructed. We only know that interest was generated by something that took place in the presentation, or by the physical nature of the presentation itself.

Finally, let us take a brief look at the domain of psychomotor behaviors. Multi-image is a useful medium for demonstrating psychomotor skills of various kinds, but the more complex the skill, and the less familiar it is to the students, the more time and practice will be necessary to attain that skill. When psychomotor skills are being learned, it is necessary to have a model of some kind. When skiing, the model might well be another skier on the hill who obviously has a high degree of expertise. On the other hand, a multi-image presentation might serve as the model if it is designed properly, and if the activity is such that the medium can be used in a practical way. If the presentation can be followed immediately by a practice session, the effectiveness of this approach will be greater than will be the case if much time elapses between presentation and practice sessions.

Once again, there is a paucity of research in this area, and most of our statements are based on observation and assumption.

In summation, the following statements can be made: Three areas of behavior are recognized; these are cognitive, affective, and psychomotor. Of the three, multi-image appears to have its greatest application in the domain of the affective, i.e., emotions. If carefully designed, the medium is useful in a restricted sense for the teaching of selected cognitive skills. Multi-image can be used in a limited way to foster psychomotor learning.

Having examined the relationship between behavior type and medium, let us now consider some of the special techniques that are associated with multi-image.

Special Techniques

1. *Combined Motion and Still Images.* Sometimes the addition of actual motion helps make a point or teach a concept. Motion pictures and stills can be combined to achieve an infinite number of effects.

2. *Panorama.* Panoramas are among the more striking displays that result from the use of multi-image. A panorama is a continuous scene that extends across the total image area (generally three screens).

3. *Atmosphere.* Related visuals can be combined and presented in such a way that a particular atmosphere is created. One such presentation on jungles used a concentra-

tion of shots of flowers, trees, streams, etc., along with an audio track of jungle sounds to create a sense of being deep in a primordial rain forest.

4. *Comparison.* In this common approach, the teacher shows the examples of an instance or object simultaneously in order to provide the opportunity for the group to observe similarities and differences. Contrasts between examples are readily seen, as are similarities and relationships.

5. *Discrimination.* A number of examples of a concept are shown along with non-examples. The student attempts to identify the examples and to classify them.

6. *Alternating Points of View.* This is the sequential or simultaneous projection of a particular object from various camera positions and distances.

7. *Sequence.* A sequential presentation displays the temporal aspects of an event in a specified order. The stages can be shown simultaneously or displayed in a cumulative manner, beginning with the first step and building up to the complete sequence.

8. *Cue Summation.* Visuals are presented that contain a selection of relevant cues which add up to a more complete comprehension of the material. A broad mix of media is often used (such as films, slides, audio, and printed material) to develop an in-depth comprehension of a concept, technique, etc.

9. *Single-Referent Emphasis.* Identical slides can be shown using a variety of techniques. For example, a given image can be projected repeatedly on the same screen; or, it might be shown randomly on different ones; or, the same image might be shown simultaneously on all screens. The idea here is to load the senses with a given referent to make a point or to develop a certain emotional state in the viewer.

10. *Testing and Review.* A wide range of testing and/or review techniques is available to the teacher who uses multi-image. One simple, yet effective, technique is to display

the problem on one screen and the solution on another. A review technique that works well consists of showing sequentially the steps in solving a particular problem.

11. *Center of Interest.* You can borrow from the artist's principles of composition to create a definite center of interest in a multiple screen display. If you wish to direct attention to a single aspect of a complex visual array, you can use color, or directing devices such as "leading lines," position on the screen, size, etc. For example, when a colored slide is displayed with equivalent black-and-white ones, it will be the colored visual that generally attracts the initial attention.

12. *Zooms.* If you have access to a slide copier, you can take a series of successively closer exposures of a given slide which, when shown in rapid succession across the screens, gives the effect of a zoom-in. The opposite approach gives the effect of a zoom-out.

13. *Varied Format and Position.* It is a relatively simple matter to change the format of a slide from the standard rectangular two to three proportion. Masks made from Kodalith film in various shapes and sizes are combined with the slide to project a uniquely-shaped image onto the screen. Additionally, the position of the visuals in relation to one another can be varied on the screens. Half-frame and vertical slides make it possible to arrange the images in a wide variety of combinations.

14. *Image Emphasis.* A slide may be displayed for any length of time desired to give viewers a chance for in-depth, detailed examination. Also, peripheral information can be displayed around the theme slide. Or, graphic arrows, pointing hands, key words, etc., may be employed as supplementary devices aloi g with the theme slide.

15. *Simulated Motion.* Motion can be actual (as in a motion picture), or it can be simulated. Slides that are properly sequenced and designed can be changed rapidly to accomplish a kind of animation.

As you work with the medium, you will come up with special effects of your own, many of which will be unique to your specific operation.

5.

The Audience

Multi-image is particularly well-received by young people. The fast pace, the ever-changing images, the saturation of color and sound, and the emotional impact combine to form an experience that is suited to the youthful temperament. Adults seem less inclined to relate to multi-image presentations if the treatment is too "far-out." This attitude is most likely a manifestation of the psychological make-up of most older persons. As one middle-aged person was heard to say during a recent multi-image festival, "I wish that they would slow it down, it simply moves too fast for me." This sums up the feeling that seems to be fairly common among older audiences. But this cannot be the total reason for the differences in preference among groups. It has been suggested that the younger audiences are more "visually literate" than are the older ones. They have been reared in a period that is characterized by the simultaneous presentation of multiple images and sounds from a variety of sources. This situation has enabled them, or forced them, as the case may be, to learn to contend with a communication problem that is unique in the human experience. Not only can the young people attend to and interpret more signals than can the older folk, but they are also more efficient at switching channels and filtering out inputs that are deemed to be of secondary value—at least, this is what the theory holds.

It would be most useful and interesting if studies were to be undertaken that would examine the contentions noted above. Lacking such studies, we have the advice of experts in the field to fall back on, and they suggest the following as criteria that should be used in planning for the utilization of multi-image.

The length of a presentation should be shorter for younger audiences. Although youthful groups find the approach to be highly interesting and motivating, they still tend to suffer from a short attention span. An optimal length is from 15 to 30 minutes, although presentations of up to two hours, if well-planned and executed, can be used with more mature audiences.

The factor of captive vs. mobile audiences should be considered. An audience that will be in one place for a given length of time presents the operator with fewer problems than does the audience that is made up of individuals who move about freely. For the latter kind of group, the presentation may have to be of rather short duration, and cycled over and over again. Obviously, most presentations that are designed for use with student groups are of the former variety.

You should prepare the audience for the presentation by helping them to develop a set for what is to come. This is most important if the presentation has a cognitively-based orientation. A simple overview might suffice; or, if time permits, an in-depth coverage of content using more traditional teaching methods may be useful. If the presentation is affectively-based, you may simply wish to "spring it" on the students. This approach will work best if the students have had some prior exposure to multi-image. For those who are total neophytes, you may find that a short explanation of the mechanics of the medium will be useful. There have been instances in which first-time audiences became so enamored with the technique that they spent more time looking at the equipment and the operators than at the presentation on the screens.

At the conclusion of the presentation, you may wish to ask the students to comment on their impressions. If the presentation is a first-time effort, it will probably be full of "bugs," but it will very likely look good to you because of your extensive involvement with it. The students can pick out the parts that fail to come across and communicate to them. Often, the criticisms are of sequences that you think are strong, and the accolades will be directed toward those segments that you had doubts about. Trust your audience— they have a degree of objectivity that you, as producer, can never quite attain due to your investment in the production. Don't be too remorseful if you must toss out more than you care to; your presentation will be the better for it.

If the presentation has a cognitive orientation, testing can be undertaken using whatever strategy is deemed suitable. Psychologists who deal with tests and measurements suggest that the form of the test should reflect the manner in which the learning took place. This is, of course, almost impossible to accomplish when the multi-image format is used as the major instructional element. However, if the information that was taught tended to be highly visual in nature, perhaps some kind of test using visuals, rather than the traditional words-only approach, could be improvised.

At any rate, students frequently seem rather drained at the conclusion of a heavily-loaded multi-image session, and some benefit might be realized if a delayed test were given. Such a delay would enable the students to organize in their minds, if not on paper, the mass of information that was proffered them.

6.

Planning the Presentation

At the very onset, it should be recognized that multi-image production isn't for everyone. You may want to develop a presentation, but there are several prerequisites that must be considered before such an effort is initiated. You must ask yourself the following questions:

1. Do I have the expertise and knowledge to create and present the program?
2. Is the equipment available not only to produce the program, but also to present it?
3. Will I have the time to do what I wish to do?
4. Are materials such as film, graphics supplies, etc., available, or do I feel that I can afford to purchase them?
5. Is there a suitable facility in which I can show the program once it has been completed?

This publication will be of value in certain of the areas mentioned above, but it can do little to help resolve such problems as lack of time and money. If, after due consideration, you are determined to forge ahead, you must have some kind of an idea around which to build the presentation before you can get underway.

The Idea

Sometimes, ideas evolve subconsciously as you go about

the task of presenting a lesson that has come to be somewhat routine for you. Often, in a flash of insight, the vision of an exciting multi-image modification of the lesson comes to you. At other times, it is a matter of sitting down and doggedly working at the problem in a logical, step-by-step fashion. There seems to be no single, cut-and-dried formula for coming up with a good idea, but you must have one before you can proceed to the next steps in the sequence.

One approach that might be useful is to involve your students in the process of conceiving, planning, producing, and presenting the presentation. If you can manage to do so, you should make arrangements for the group to view a multi-image presentation before you do anything else. In some areas, this might be a problem; but where such programs are available, this is an excellent way in which to acquaint your group with the medium. After the students have a concept of what the medium is, you might outline some of the areas within a subject field that you feel would be suitable for this approach. Given these broad guidelines, the students can then collectively come up with more concrete ideas that will lead to the formulation of objectives. Such student-centered planning tactics are eagerly embraced by those involved, but a word of caution should be extended at this point. In their enthusiasm, the students more often than not come up with ideas that are beyond their ability to carry out. You will most likely find it necessary to interject some calm objectivity into the planning session to insure the ultimate success of the project.

The Objectives

Once the idea has been established, you can begin to look at potential objectives. You should ask yourself what the ultimate effect on the audience is to be. Or, put another way, what it is that you would have your audience do or experience as a result of having viewed the program.

There are differing points of view relative to the framing of objectives. One school holds that they should be narrowly prescribed, while the "humanistic" school advocates a loosely-structured approach. Regardless of how you personally feel about objectives, it is necessary that somehow you deal with this requirement. One of the problems relating to objectives and multi-image is that many of the behaviors associated with this medium are affective in nature, and affective behaviors present us with the greatest difficulties in the writing of objectives. So, in spite of your best intentions, it may be that you will have to settle for general statements where presentations that deal with emotional kinds of things are concerned. On the other hand, if the acquisition of knowledge is the main goal, you can develop some specific objectives that reflect the more traditional kind of approach.

After you have come to grips with objectives, you should consider some additional points that have to do with the mechanics of the program.

The Mechanics of the Program

You should consider the length of the program, although this tends to change as production moves ahead. Experience has demonstrated that retention of factual material is greatest when the length of the presentation is relatively short. For presentations that emphasize an affective approach, a longer time-span can be used. To be more specific, a ten-minute program that is loaded with information has been found to be more effective than one of similar content that is, say, 20 minutes in length. Of course, there are many other factors that must be considered, including the age of the members of the audience.

Another consideration is that of format. Do you plan to use available pictures primarily? Or, will you have to go out on location to get the visuals? Obviously, copying from a stack of books and magazines is a much simpler matter than is going out into the community for the material. Do you plan to use motion, or will the presentation consist entirely of slides? It is easier to stay with slides, but you may need motion to convey effectively a particular concept.

Then there is the concern about screen arrangement. The typical presentation uses three, or a combination that will accommodate three projected images. If the facility is already set up, this concern is moot; otherwise, you will need to consider the problem. You may wish to have but two screens and two projectors, or, four projectors with dissolves. You may want to consider a central horizontal screen with flanking vertical ones, and so on.

What about the actual presentation of the program? You will want to begin thinking about who will be involved in this activity, when it will take place, and who the audience will be.

The Script and Storyboard

Now that the groundwork has been laid, it is time to get down to work. Typically, you are going to need a script and a storyboard, both of which take time and effort to create. There are times when the storyboard may be neither necessary nor desirable, but for the teacher working with a group of students, it is an excellent planning aid that keeps the group on target. Producers who have experience with the medium may dispense with the storyboard entirely, preferring to work directly from the script in a less structured manner. Such an approach allows for a certain amount of serendipity, and the creative person is freed from the constraints that a storyboard imposes, but the neophyte will often find such freedom to be a hindrance rather than a help.

The initial script is typically a rather rough-looking combination of typed copy, penciled corrections, pasted-in entries, and scratched-out deletions. It reflects the mental gymnastics that go into the production of an acceptable first-draft. This first-draft is then re-typed onto a format that is adaptable to the specific operational strategies of the program developer. For example, some individuals prefer a simple, straightforward script from which to make the storyboard. Spaces might be left between written sequences so that a brief description of the visuals can be written down. Others like a script that is typed in a column on half the sheet, with the other column reserved for a description of the visuals. Still others prefer to have a format that includes three (or more) boxes arranged in successive horizontal lines, with a space for the script on a line with each set of boxes. The visuals are then indicated in sketch form in each of the boxes. This type of script actually incorporates the storyboard feature, and, when the rectangles are filled with the appropriate sketches, there really is no need to worry about subsequent storyboarding.

As you write the script, you must think of yourself as a spectator, seated off to the side somewhere, watching an event unfold before your eyes. The key to writing a successful script for a predominantly visual presentation is to be able to think with images rather than with words. Oh yes, the words are generally needed, but they are different from the words that you would use if images were not present. To put it another way, imagine that you have a picture of something, but your friend in the next room has no picture. Your task is to explain to your friend as accurately as possible the appearance of that picture—it's like a game that we used to play, isn't it? Well, you will have to use all kinds of words and their modifiers in order to describe that picture, and even then, your friend will not have a totally accurate image in his or her mind. Now, walk through the door and show the picture to your friend. In an instant, he or she has an accurate impression of something that you could never totally convey with descriptive words. At this point, any lengthy description of the visual is merely redundant and unnecessary. This is the way that you should approach the task of writing a script for your presentation. The audience has the image right up there in full view; there is no reason to describe it with words. So, you might opt to let the picture alone tell the story, or, more commonly, you would have a musical accompaniment. If you should decide on some narration to go with a particular slide segment, it should be simple, concise, and appropriate, and should add something to the segment that is lacking in the pictures alone. Your motto should be: "If the pictures tell the story, forget the words."

If you plan to use a storyboard, now is an appropriate time to move to this phase. Storyboard frames are the visual equivalent of the images that will subsequently appear on the screens. A one-projector storyboard is easy to use. The illustrations, each of which represents a single slide, are sequential, like the pages in a book—one after another. Multi-image storyboards are much more complex than this, and they become particularly intricate when sophisticated programmers are used. As a matter of fact, with intricate presentations built around sophisticated programmers, story-boards may have to be of a very general nature because to attempt to specify each function graphically would be out of the question.

Various storyboard formats are available, but you may wish to create one that will serve your particular needs. If your presentation will utilize three screens, then the story-board forms should have three rectangles which repre-sent the screens. With the script in hand, you can begin to fill the rectangles with appropriate sketches. At this point, the programming considerations come into play; you cannot adequately deal with the visual sequence if you do not think in terms of the specifics of how the images are to appear on the screen. For example, you may wish to have one slide remain on the screen through three or four changes of slides on the other screens—you will have to spell this out on the storyboard, or you will encounter problems when the actual programming sequence takes place.

One of the virtues of multi-image is that the potential for special effects is so extensive. By "special effects" we mean the modification of the slide and/or the manner of presenting it. A brief description of a number of special techniques is included in the chapter on utilization. The following discussion involves a more detailed coverage of a few of these techniques.

A common effect is the dissolve sequence. Two projectors are connected to a dissolve unit, which works much like the dimmer switch in your living room. Both projectors are focused at a specific area on a given screen so that the images superimpose precisely. With one projector off, and the other one on, a single image is seen. The traditional way of getting to slide two from the first slide is to retrieve slide one and drop slide two—the result is a blank screen for a short fraction of time. The dissolve gradually fades out slide one (which is located in one projector) while bringing slide two (located in the second projector) up to full luminance. The effect is a gradual transition from the original visual to the succeeding one. This interesting effect is typically referred to as the "lap dissolve." If you plan ahead, you can create third colors from the mixture of different colors on two slides. This is generally done with graphics, that is, cards of solid colors with a title or an illustration on their surfaces. A red card fading into a yellow card gives variations of the color orange. A blue and yellow will result in green, etc. The students often come up with unusual effects of their own as they play with the dissolve feature. Another effective way to use the dissolve is to fade from a visual to complete black and vice versa through the use of blank slides.

You can also project one slide over another to achieve some attention-getting effects. This is done with two projectors that are carefully aligned to fill a given area on the

Figure 1

A low-cost dissolve unit. The rate of dissolve can be varied from one to ten seconds.

Picture courtesy Audiotronics.

Figure 2

A multi-speed dissolve control. This unit has three distinctly different dissolve speeds in addition to a number of other functions.

Picture courtesy Spindler and Sauppe.

screens. This is similar to the set-up for the dissolve sequence, but there are certain modifications. The initial slide is most often a negative slide (such as Kodalith) with white letters or other graphic materials on a black ground. Initially, the effect is one of a traditional-looking image on the screen—nothing unusual about it, but the second, or negative, slide makes the difference. As this image falls upon the screen, the effect is one of white or colored words or figures that "drop out" of the screen image. The reason such a dual slide combination works is that the light passing through the captions on the negative slide combines with the light that is already on the screen to give this restricted area a double shot of light, thereby causing the words, etc., to show as light areas against the image on the screen.

If you have the resources, you can use three projectors for each screen to achieve an effect such as described but with a dissolve thrown in. Two of the projectors are connected to the dissolve unit, while the third contains the negative caption slides. As the visuals dissolve one into another, the captions pop up at appropriate times. One can see easily how such an approach can be used for the teaching of cognitive information. You might have a question on one screen, with the answer on another. Or, you might have drop-out arrows with labels that point to the parts of an object. Many uses for this technique can be developed by the creative multi-image producer.

It is possible to create an effect of animation if the visuals are carefully conceived. One way in which to do this is to change the slides in rapid succession from screen to screen. One example of a simple approach occurs when identical slides of an object, say a car, are placed in each of the three projectors. The projector that contains the slide with the front of the car facing projector number two is activated first—this makes the car move in the proper direction. After a brief glimpse, the slide is retrieved and a blank slide drops;

the middle slide is rapidly revealed and retrieved; and the same with projector three. The effect is of a car speeding across the screens. This is a rather simple approach to animation, but it is a way to get started. Let's consider a more sophisticated technique. Now, we take several shots of a runner with our motor-driven camera (if one is available). The resulting slides will show the legs in various sequential attitudes, much as a movie would do, but with interim frames missing. We can use these slides in the same fashion as we used the car slides, but the effect will be more striking because the legs, arms, and body stance will change from screen to screen—thus giving an acceptable illusion of movement.

You can make a train roar down the track right into the audience by taking a series of slides that show the sequential size increase of the train as it approaches. You might use your standard camera (if you don't have a motor-drive) to take the pictures of a train that is moving slowly. The effect is speeded up enormously in the projection process, and the train rushes down the track at breakneck speed. It should be noted that professional multi-image presentations typically employ more than the standard three projectors for the animation sequences.

One of the more spectacular applications of the multi-screen technique is the panorama. It consists of a common scene that extends across all three screens. The technique for creating a panorama is described in the production section of this book.

Once you are aware of the techniques that can be applied to the sequencing of visuals, you are ready to cue the script. Note that on the sample storyboard-script (see Appendix A), provisions have been made for indicating which of the projectors is to be activated. Merely filling in one of the cue spots provided indicates which of the programmer keys is to be pressed. It should be noted that this type of storyboard-script is most useful when tone-control programmers are being used. Since most schools and media centers that have programmers will have this type, it seems appropriate to emphasize the kind of storyboard-script that is illustrated. But, what do you do if you lack a programmer of any kind? You can still have your show. Use the same storyboard and fill in the cue spots in the same manner, but do this with three different colors. Now, tape the remote advances from the three projectors side by side to a board, and color each of these with colors that correspond to the cue spots. By following the script, you will be able to activate the projectors on cue, and you will have your multi-image show—but, more on this later.

As you work through the storyboard-script, you should indicate in the rectangles the effect that is to be seen on the screen. There are many ways to do this, but a good approach is to draw a cross through the slides that are blank, draw a simple sketch in those that represent image slides, and draw a vertical arrow from a rectangle to the one below for a "hold." Note that the rectangles are lined up in the same order, as will be the projectors on the stands. Of course, the real concern is that the trays of slides always end up on the proper projectors, so it is necessary that these be identified in some manner. One possibility is to use numbers or letters, or a combination of these, for presentations that use multiple projectors for each screen and "a" to designate the first projector on screen number one. We will take another look at loading and identifying trays later in this book, in the section on using the light table and traying slides.

7.

Producing the Presentation

The multi-image programs that are produced by professionals involve techniques that require specialized, expensive equipment that is not available to classroom teachers and their "production team" of students. But this fact should not discourage you from getting involved with the medium at a different level. It is possible to combine existing slides and other materials such as audio-cassettes into the multi-image format, thus avoiding much of the initial production effort. Such an approach might be fine for a first run, but sooner or later you will want to be more directly involved in the production aspects. The simplest option is to use available equipment, such as the ubiquitous Instamatic in the 126 slide format. You can use the little 110s also, but the size is less compatible with the standard 35mm than is the 126.

For copy work, use the Kodak Ektagraphic Visualmaker with the Instamatic camera. This device has two copy stands with built-in close-up lenses that permit you to take pictures of graphics and other materials that are too small to be photographed with a normal lens.

On the other hand, if you have a 35mm camera with the proper features, you are in even better shape. The camera should be of the single-lens reflex type, and you will need a macro lens or extension tubes for close-up work. You can build your own copy stand using plans that are available from

Kodak, or, you might purchase an inexpensive one. A pair of flood lamps completes the set-up; choose lamps that are compatible with the film that you plan to use.

There may be times when you will find it necessary to copy some slides. This process is referred to as "duplicating," and the product is often called a "dupe." You can't simply lay the slides out on the copy stand and photograph them as you can your opaque materials; you must illuminate them by passing light through them. In a pinch, slides can be projected onto a screen, and then this image can be photographed, but the best technique involves copying the illuminated slide directly. Slide copiers of varying degrees of sophistication are available. The simplest models look like long tubes that fit on the camera in place of the lens. The slide is inserted in a special holder that is located on the forward end of the tube. Such copying devices typically require a light source of considerable magnitude—merely pointing out the window as you would do with the normal lens on the camera is normally not sufficient.

Then there are the sophisticated copiers. These have a light source built into them, and they provide a number of features that range all the way from cropping the image to color correcting. Specifics relating to the use of such equipment generally are provided by the media specialist who is in charge of such things. Also, complete, descriptive literature on the operation of the copier should be available in the facility. Additionally, most commercial processors provide a slide duplicating service for those who desire it. This is a bit expensive, but necessary, if you have exhausted all of your other options.

If you plan to create your own titles or graphics, make them conform to the proportions of the 35mm slide, which is two units high to three units wide. Using three inches as the unit, you would obtain an area six inches by nine inches. Using four inches as the unit, you would have an eight by 12

Figure 3

A slide duplicator set-up. This unit can be used to enlarge 110 and 126 to the 35mm format, and to reduce large slides down to the 35mm format.

Picture courtesy Impact Communications, Inc.

Figure 4

A slide duplicator. This unit is used for duplicating slides, creating zoom sequences, cropping, color correcting, background tinting, and other techniques.

Picture courtesy Radmar, Inc.

format, etc. Leave some unused space around the art work, that is, do not letter or draw right out to the edges of the card. When the art work fills the entire card, a certain amount of the image is frequently lost during the act of photographing it; or, more commonly, the edges of the card will show up in the slide. Leaving a blank margin all the way around the lettering or illustration will help you to solve this problem.

Lettering

If you need some lettering, you have a number of ways in which to achieve just about any desired effect. Dry-transfer letters give a professional look to captions and titles. Such lettering is available from art and audiovisual outlets in a wide range of styles and sizes. Applying the letters is a simple process; simply position the sheet of letters so that the letter to be transferred is in the desired position on the art work. Then, rub the letter with a blunt instrument such as a burnisher or even a dull pencil—the letter will release from the backing sheet and will then transfer to the art work.

Or, you might use the die-cut letter for large, simple titles. Such letters are punched from a sheet of paper or plastic and, typically, have an adhesive backing. They are available from a number of sources, including variety stores, art outlets, etc.

Mechanical lettering devices are easy to use, and produce quick, clean lettering. Check your media center for devices such as the scriber and template or pen and guide sets. Most such systems have the directions for use attached to the lid of the case; many books on graphic production give directions on how to use mechanical lettering devices. With a bit of practice, you should become quite proficient at lettering with this kind of equipment.

Other, more esoteric kinds of lettering equipment are also available in some educational settings where specialized jobs of various kinds are performed. The photoprinter uses a matrix that consists of letter negatives, a light source, and a developing solution to produce clean, sharp lettering on photographic film or paper. Other devices, such as the Leteron system, stamp letters from a roll of colored tape-like material. Hot presses stamp foil letters onto cards for use in TV production, and so on.

Graphics

Graphics—that is, diagrams, cartoons, illustrations, etc.— can be rendered in a number of ways. You might purchase books of "clip art," the contents of which can be cut apart and reassembled on the art card. Use rubber cement or a wax-coater to attach the elements to the card. Or, you can trace parts or all of an illustration onto a sheet, and then add any additional details that you deem to be necessary. Use a good grade of tracing paper, or a vellum, and India ink for nice, contrasty effects. Small sable brushes are excellent for such work, but pens are preferred by many. If ink frightens you, then a fine black marker can be used.

The finished art card, which is a combination of a number of elements, serves as the basis for the slides that will become the visual components of the multi-image presentation. For more specific information on the creation of such cards, refer to books that are devoted to the area of graphic production.

Photography

With the lettering and the art work finished, and the other visual materials selected and arranged, the time has come to think about photography. It would be well at this point to mention some of the more important requirements that lead to the production of a good slide.

When using a color reversal film, make sure that the light source is compatible with the film. This information, along with information on filters for conversion to other light sources, is contained in the literature that comes with the film. Use polarizing filters over the lights and camera lens to control the saturation of color. By manipulating the filters, you can achieve a richness of color that is not possible under normal conditions.

Watch for "hot spots" on your art work. If these appear in the viewfinder, you can be assured that the film will pick them up. When a film such as Kodalith is being used, the effect is one of unequal development across the film surface. This generally can be corrected during processing if the tray method and red light illumination are used; but, at times, fine details will be lost. You can prevent reflections by turning out any overhead lights, using non-glare glass as a cover sheet for the art work, and masking the camera with a piece of black paper through which a hole has been punched to accommodate the lens. This last trick is one that is often overlooked. It is made necessary by the glaring chrome surfaces of many cameras—chrome-finish cameras are attractive, but they give off reflections that are often picked up by the glossy surfaces of pictures that are being copied.

If possible, photograph everything under the same light source. This is frequently not practical, particularly if you are combining slides from a number of different sources. It is quite important to have slides that are consistent in color fidelity and value when multi-image is being used, given the potential for comparison. The linear feature of the single screen presentation makes it a bit easier to use visuals that vary somewhat as to quality, but when several images are simultaneously available, any discrepancies, no matter how small, are quite evident.

Use a level of some kind to line up the camera so that it is parallel to the art work. This will prevent the occurrence of distortion that can be quite noticeable, especially where straight lines and lettering are being copied.

Now, if you are ready to proceed with the copy work, you

will need the right kind of film. If the work to be copied is "line copy," you can use a high-contrast line film for the job. Line copy is identified by its lack of intermediate values; that is, it is either black or it is white, and there is nothing in between. For best results, use a high-contrast copy film, such as Kodalith Ortho film 6556, type 3. This film is available in 100 foot rolls at a very modest price. Some photo outlets are now making this film available in 20 and 36 exposure cassette loads.

With the 35mm camera on the copy stand, make a test strip using one of your black-and-white art cards as the subject. The ASA or light sensitivity rating of Kodalith is very low, about 6, so you will find it necessary to use long exposure times in order to obtain satisfactory results. Take a meter reading, then increase and decrease the exposure time using the smallest available aperture setting on the camera. You will obtain a strip of film that has one frame exposed exactly at the meter reading, several frames exposed at successively faster shutter speeds, and several frames exposed at successively slower speeds. You may find that exposures of one or two seconds, or even longer, give the best results. If, as is the case with some cameras, your light meter does not have a sufficiently slow ASA designation to accommodate the litho film, bypass the meter and run a test strip with the camera set at the smallest f-setting and the shutter speeds varied up and down from a setting of one second.

After the film has been exposed, process it according to the directions, and determine which of all of the frames is the best one—this will enable you to select the one optimum exposure setting for all subsequent slides.

Since Kodalith is a negative-type film, your slides will be reversals of the original art work. In many cases, such negative slides can be used as they are with considerable effectiveness, or, you may wish to add a touch of color to them. One way to add color is to mount a small slice of colored plastic with the negative slide. The preferred plastics are the theatrical varieties, which are referred to as "gels," but you can get by with nothing more than a section from a colored plastic theme-binder, or even a piece of cellophane.

A more permanent way in which to color the slides is to use a dye, which is applied with a "Q-Tip" or similar applicator. Some excellent permanent felt-tipped markers are available that work about as well as dye and are simple to use. Apply the colors with care, since they tend to streak a bit. Colors should be applied to the emulsion side of the film, since this is the side that will absorb the most dye; however, if you desire a more saturated effect, it is feasible to apply the dye to both the base and the emulsion sides of the film.

After the color has been applied, you should check the negative slide very carefully for any imperfections that must be blocked out. At times, the edges of cut-outs (such as clip art) will show up on the slide as a thin, white line. At other times, pinholes and other small spots that are generally a by-product of incorrect exposure or processing tend to crop up. Most of these problems can be resolved by applying an opaque solution directly over the imperfection with a fine, pointed brush. The opaque solution is a heavy red paste that can be completely removed from the film surface with water. As a general rule, the opaque is applied to the base side of the film. This is important if you plan to make a positive slide from the negative, but it is not critical if you will use the negative strictly as a projected slide.

When making a positive slide from the negative, the following steps are recommended: First, cut the strip of negatives into sections that are four or five frames in length. Strips that are longer than this are difficult to handle. Now, cut a section of 35mm Kodalith stock that is slightly longer than the strip of negatives that you plan to use. Next, sandwich the negatives and film together, emulsion to emulsion, and place them over a black sheet of paper.

Position a piece of clean glass over this to hold the films firmly in place. A light is now turned on to expose the film—a good technique is to use an enlarger for this purpose, although a regular tungsten lamp will work. Remove the exposed film and process it; you now have a positive image which can be used as is, or can be colored or treated in other ways as desired.

Incidentally, all processing of Kodalith film can be conducted under a red light source, since the film, being orthochromatic, is not sensitive to the red band of the spectrum.

The above discussion involved the use of black-and-white, high-contrast, negative films. What about color-reversal films? Obviously, we would use such films when copying materials such as photographs in books, original continuous-tone art work, and actual objects. However, such film is not suitable for copying paste-up work such as that described above. Every seam, every spot of rubber cement, every layout pencil line will pick up on the slide, and the result will be unsatisfactory. This doesn't mean that techniques cannot be employed to make the direct copy of titles and graphics practical. For example, transfer or die-cut letters on a colored card make an attractive title when copied onto a reversal color film, such as Ektachrome; but it should be remembered that the effect will be much different from that obtained with a high-contrast line film.

Slide Masks

At some point in time, you will most likely tire of the square or rectangular slide format and will want to try some variations. The simplest way in which to change the format of the slide is to use the commercial masks that are available in a number of designs. These are bound in a mount along with the slide; the slide can then be used as is, or it can be recopied with a slide copier. Or, you can make your own masks by cutting a shape from black construction paper and photographing it on Kodalith film. The result will be a clear window on an opaque ground; once again, this is mounted together with the image slide.

A different approach involves the use of a special matte box that mounts on the front of the slide camera. The box, which is much like a cubical bellows, has a mask holder at the front which accommodates a full range of masks that can be quickly slipped in and out as needs change. A mask consists of an opaque or colored sheet of plastic or cardboard which has an opening cut through it. The opening can assume any of an infinite number of shapes, but the most common ones are based on standard figures, such as hearts, circles, stars, etc. The photograph is taken through the opening, the edges of which are out of focus so that a soft outline effect is obtained.

Special Slide Effects

Special effects filters/lenses can be used to create unique modifications in the photographic image. For example, there is the multiple-image prism, which fits over the standard 35mm lens. This device is so constructed that the image is repeated in a variety of patterns on the slide. The image might be repeated three or four times in a straight line, or, there might be a central image with several identical images clustered around it. Some of these multiple-image lenses are adjustable, enabling you to modify the number and position of the duplicated images by merely twisting the lens component.

Then there is the filter that loads the slide with spectral colors. The structure of this filter is such that it acts like a cluster of miniature prisms, effectively breaking the light into its component colors, and concentrating these in various areas of the slide.

You might also be interested in soft, foggy, or misty

effects for certain purposes. By using a filter ·that is made specifically for this purpose, you can create an "out-of-this-world" atmosphere even with the most mundane of subject matter.

For a quick vignette effect, a special lens is available that diffuses the edges of the picture while leaving the central area sharply in focus. Such lenses simply screw into the normal camera lens like any ordinary filter.

Star filters are quite popular with those who desire an image that is normal in most respects, but has spectacular highlights that have the appearance of long-ray stars. You can purchase star filters that have as few as four points or rays, or variations that involve a great number of these and look like a sunburst.

Another interesting filter is the one that enables you to create the effect of motion in a still picture. The slide will appear as if the picture, or a portion thereof, was taken at a slow shutter speed—that is, portions of the objects will appear blurred or streaked. The advantages that the filter enjoys over a technique involving a slow speed and moving subject are that a perfectly still object can be made to appear as if it were moving, and you can selectively control the movement effect as you compose the picture.

The panorama shot should be mentioned, as long as we are on the subject of special effects. This technique involves the use of the multiple screens to display a single scene across the total area. Although spectacular in appearance, the panorama is tricky to create without special equipment, because perfect registration between the three segments of the scene (the three matched slides) becomes difficult. To solve the problem, manufacturers have developed a device called a "panorama head." This fits on a tripod, with the camera attached to it. The head is leveled, and the entire set-up is securely stationed so that movement, other than a horizontal sweep, is prevented.

Professional heads have indexing points that make the coordination of the three exposures very accurate. If you lack such equipment, you might try the "eye balling" approach. You will still need the tripod, but you cannot lock the camera to it, because this will prevent the lateral movement that you will need to get three adjacent views. Give the camera just enough play that you can pivot from one extreme point to the other. You will have to use visual reference points to help establish the three camera positions—it is tricky, but with some practice, satisfactory panoramas are a possibility.

Mounting the Slides

When the films are finally processed, colored, etc., they must be mounted. Cardboard mounts are inexpensive and easy to use. They are very light in weight and, when in good shape, work well in the 140-slide Carousel trays. They tend to become ragged and bent with use, however, and thus do not feed as well as they would if new. Also, such mounts have been known to come apart due to failure of the heat seal. This problem can be corrected easily, but if it occurs during a show, the slide is likely to jam in the projector.

Plastic mounts are more substantial than are the paper ones, and they tend to hold up better. The more expensive ones are called "pin-register mounts." These have square pins that fit the sprocket holes of the film, thus securing it in position in a highly positive fashion. The pin mount is an excellent choice if you have some precision slide alignment with which you are concerned. Plastic mounts have problems, too. Some are too bulky to work in the 140 trays, so you would find it necessary to limit the tray size to the 80-slide variety. Some plastic mounts are not completely opaque—a feature that affects the aesthetic quality of the presentation.

Both of the mount types mentioned above are termed "open-frame," and the glass mount is a "closed-frame" variety. Open-frame mounts tend to cool better than the closed ones, but they afford less protection to the film itself. Glass mounts are also easy to clean, and their weight causes them to work better (to drop more reliably) in the Carousel projectors. However, most won't work in the 140 tray, and they cost significantly more than do the other two varieties. You should carefully consider your specific needs, and then look at the pros and cons of the various types of mounts that are available.

With the slides finished and mounted, you will now have to arrange and sequence them; this calls for the use of the light box or table.

Using the Light Table

The light table or light box consists of a frame, within which a bank of fluorescent lights is located, and a top sheet of frosted glass or plastic. You can purchase such equipment from an art supply store (can be expensive) or from a photo equipment outlet (also expensive) or, at times, from a surplus government supplies agency (light boxes from this source are generally quite small in size). Or, you might make your own light box. All that you need for this is a wooden frame of some kind, a piece of translucent plastic sheeting or surplus frosted glass, and a fluorescent light fixture. Attach the fixture flush within the frame, and fasten the sheet over the top. For a simple, quick job, use wide tape and merely tape the sheet in place. With a felt marker, draw vertical and horizontal sets of lines that duplicate the position of the boxes on your storyboard—be sure that the boxes on the glass are large enough to accommodate a two-inch by two-inch slide with some space to spare. Or, you might use thin tape, such as Chart Pak, to make the lines. Make as many three-box columns as will fit on the light table; leave a space between each set of boxes. The three boxes represent the three screens, and you should place the slides in the boxes in precisely the same way as you wish to have them appear on the screens.

Now, for the first time, you will actually see what the final presentation will look like in a static sense—the motion is missing, but the visuals are all there, laid out in sequence and lighted so that you can study them individually and collectively. At this point, some of the slides will appear to be out of sequence, or there will be holes that need to be plugged with additional slides. Trim some two-inch by two-inch blanks of paper, and write a description of the needed visual on the blank. Place this in the proper place on the table right along with the slides. After you have progressed through the complete presentation, go back and deal with each one of the blanks, creating the art work, taking the photographs, etc., until all have been completed. Place the resulting slides in the proper places in the program and run through it again as a final double-check. Remember to include blank slides for those portions of a sequence where the screen will be black, and omit slides where a "hold" is being used.

Now, you are finally ready to tray the slides; this is mainly a matter of picking them up in the right order from the table and placing them in the trays.

Traying the Slides

If you are using three projectors only (no dissolves), you merely line up the trays to correspond with the three boxes on the table and insert the slides in the proper trays. Remember, to achieve proper slide orientation on the screen, hold the slide up in your hand, and look through it—it should be "right-reading," that is, it should look just like the original copy or object from which it was made. Now, turn the slide over so that it is upside-down and place a mark in the upper right-hand corner (the "thumb mark"); drop the slide into the tray in this position. Actually, all of this should have taken place during the light table session, and you should be able to tray the slides without having to worry about orientation, if you have done your homework.

However, if you plan to use dissolves, you will need two trays for each screen, rather than one, as mentioned above. The sequence now goes like this: slide number one in tray one, slide number two in tray two, slide number three in tray one, slide number four in tray two, etc. So, tray one will contain slides 1, 3, 5, 7, etc., while tray two will contain slides 2, 4, 6, 8, etc.

As mentioned earlier, you should identify the trays in some way so that they don't get mixed up. If you have a straight three-projector, three-screen presentation, you might simply number the trays 1, 2, 3, or A, B, C. For dissolves, where two projectors per screen are to be used, you might use the designations 1a, 1b, 2a, 2b, etc. When three projectors per screen are to be used (two dissolve projectors and one that supers), you could simply add to the designations used above.

If a rear-view screen will be used, the slides must be reversed in order that the images will be properly oriented as the audience views them. Special mirrored devices are available that automatically reverse the images when the rear-screen mode is employed. This means that it isn't necessary to manually flip each and every slide prior to using the rear-screen approach.

Remember, when a screen is to be black, you should tray an opaque slide; also, place opaque slides in the first slot in each of the trays. This enables you to turn the projectors on while maintaining the blank screens. Otherwise, when you activate the projectors, the screens will be flooded with light but will be imageless until the first image slides fall.

There is, however, an exception to this. When dissolve units are used, only one of the two trays involved for each screen needs to have an initial opaque slide. This is so because only one of the two projectors will be "on" at the start of your program; consequently, the second or "off" projector needs no blank slide.

Sound

The audio portion of the multi-image presentation shouldn't be tacked on as an afterthought. Appropriate music, words, and sound effects enhance the visuals, and often spell the difference between a program that is average and one that is "great." So, choose the audio carefully, devoting as much care to this aspect of the presentation as to the selection and creation of the visuals.

Music and special audio effects help to establish a mood that makes the audience more receptive to the program as a whole. A search through available musical selections will provide you with just about any kind of "mood music" that you might need. The thunderstorm over the Grand Canyon requires one kind of musical accompaniment, while the soaring gull requires another. Find a patriotic piece to go with the unfurled flags, and locate an idyllic score for those slides of the deer in the deep woods.

A musical selection that contains appropriate lyrics can reinforce the images, if it is carefully coordinated with them. At times, multi-image producers start with a vague and general idea (such as making a statement against war and violence) which they put to music even before they create the visuals. This atypical approach is contrary to that which is most often employed, but it points up the important role that audio can play in the presentation.

This isn't to say that every presentation must be loaded with sounds in order to be effective. It is conceivable that a multi-image show might be totally silent and still be informative and entertaining. Decisions relating to the use of sound are typically of a subjective nature and made on a personal basis.

When the objective is to teach cognitive material, you will most likely emphasize the narration while avoiding too much music. On the other hand, when the orientation is toward an affective emphasis, you will probably take the opposite approach.

Once the decision has been made to build in an audio component, you should obtain the proper equipment for the job. If a programmer is to be used, then a stereo recorder that has separate record levers for each of the two channels is needed. This feature permits the sound to be recorded on one track while the signals are recorded on the other one. We are referring to the tone-control programmer, which is the kind that is most widely available to people in education. If you should be fortunate enough to have access to a more sophisticated programmer, your selection of sound equipment might be different. Once again, if you plan to have your students operate the program manually, then any kind of recorder or tape deck will work.

Locating sources for sound effects and music that are appropriate to your specific needs can be quite a task. The problem is compounded by copyright regulations. Most music stores can give you information as to what music is available and the basis upon which it is available. Some companies produce music for the express purpose of serving the media market. You can obtain tapes and records of sound effects from various companies for a reasonable cost, or, you and your students can tape your own effects right at the source. Older, more skilled students can often be asked to improvise musical scores, and such an approach completely avoids copyright problems.

A valuable option that should be mentioned is the music library. Composers and musicians are hired with the express purpose of putting together a collection of varying selections that give the media producer a wide choice of background music. This production music is recorded in segments that

Figure 5

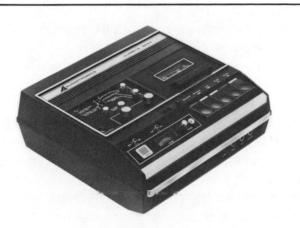

A cassette recorder that can control two projectors. Signals are added or deleted on a sync track that is separate from the sound track.

Picture courtesy Audiotronics.

cover the full gamut of media needs, ranging all the way from the epic introductory segment through mood music to the glittering finale. You can select segments that seem appropriate, and, by joining these together, can compose your own music and make it fit your unique needs.

Music libraries furnish catalogs that contain extensive listings from which to choose the specific sounds that you desire. For more information, contact one or all of the following libraries: Emil Ascher, Inc., 666 Fifth Ave., New York, NY 10036; MusiCues Corporation, 1156 Avenue of the Americas, New York, NY 10036; Corelli Jacobs Film Music, Inc., and DeWolfe Music Library, Inc., 25 West 45th Street, New York, NY 10036; and Thomas J. Valentino, Inc., 151 West 46th Street, New York, NY 10036.

For information on music that is available for use in media presentations, write to: ASCAP, 1 Lincoln Plaza, New York, NY 10023.

For an in-depth coverage of music libraries, see: "Music on Cue," by Elinor Stecker, in the October, 1979 issue of *Photomethods.*

The music, narration, and sound effects are all mixed together and recorded on the tape. There are different ways to accomplish this, but the preferred way is to use a mixer. A simple, battery-operated mixing unit is available for about $50.00 and will do a fair job. If the more sophisticated mixers are available, you will find that they afford you much greater versatility and control, especially in situations when the strength of the sounds from the different sources varies greatly.

Some options to the use of the mixer are available, but these can be cumbersome. For example, you might assemble the various audio components that go into the finished, mixed product and then feed them all simultaneously onto the tape through a microphone. This is a useful experience for students, but the quality will definitely be inferior to the product that is obtained through the use of the mixer.

Then, you might use the "voice-over" approach. In this case, you use one track of the stereo tape for the narration and the other for music. Record one of the tracks first (preferably the narration), then, as you listen to the initial sound, record the second track. Control the volume according to your desires so that the two tracks blend together nicely. Use a "Y" adapter to dub the two sound tracks onto a single one, thus "mixing" them together.

Some recorders have a "sound-on-sound" feature. Such a feature makes possible the composite recording from left channel to right channel and vice versa. Triple or more composite recordings can be made through the use of this feature.

The owner's manual that accompanies the recorder outlines the exact procedure that the operator must follow in order to accomplish the sound-on-sound effect.

Figure 6

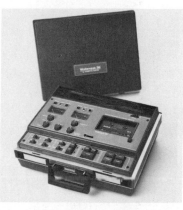

A stereo visual sync recorder that combines high fidelity sound with visual sync capabilities for multi-image presentations.

Picture courtesy Wollensak/3M Company.

The initial recording on the stereo recorder or deck is done in the stereo mode (using both channels). However, when the final tape is made, the right channel receives the tones that activate the projectors, while the left channel receives the audio. It is necessary to transfer the material that has been recorded in the stereo mode onto the left channel of a second tape to be used in the program. To accomplish this, the "Y" adapter is used. It feeds from the two stereo tracks to the left track of the second recorder. Be certain that you use tape that is new or that has been completely cleared of any previously recorded material. It is not uncommon to have residual signals on a re-recorded tape serve as advance signals that trigger the projectors at odd times—nothing is more frustrating than trying to find those hidden culprits.

Plan to experiment with your equipment before you approach the serious business of putting the sound in its final form. The stereo tape recorder can be a rather formidable device, and you will only come to know it through hands-on experience with it.

Programming

Many, if not most, of the programmers that are available to educators are of the tone-control variety. Different tones are recorded onto one of the tracks of a stereo tape, while the audio is recorded onto the other one. Such recorders are simple in concept and easy to use as well as reliable. Merely punching the proper combination of keys in accordance with the directions on the storyboard or script programs the tape. A tone-control programmer that controls three channels generates tones of three different frequencies, which are recorded on the right track of the stereo tape. During the actual presentation, the signals are fed back through the programmer, where they are interpreted and routed through the proper channel to the specific projector. In cases where the dissolve unit is used, the signal is routed to this, and the projectors that are connected to the specific unit are activated in turn.

A more sophisticated option to the tone-control programmer is the punched-tape variety. In this case, signals are encoded on a strip of tape in the form of holes that are punched through it. Various combinations of holes are used to activate the different pieces of equipment in specific ways to achieve a desired effect on the screen.

Programmers that are built around the microcomputer have capabilities that less sophisticated programmers cannot begin to approach. Such devices work much like their big brothers, storing information in a memory bank in the form of digital "bits." This means that you can try a particular effect, which can then be stored for future recall, freeing you to work on other aspects of a presentation. If any or all of the stored effects are deemed to be suitable, they can be

Figure 7

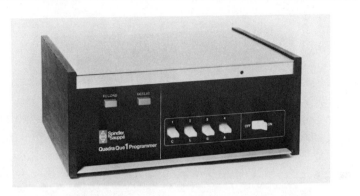

A tone-control or magnetic tape-type programmer. It encodes and decodes four discrete frequencies onto one track of the audiotape.

Picture courtesy Spindler and Sauppe.

Figure 8

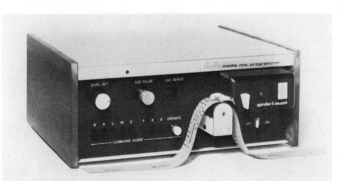

A punched-tape programmer with 27 channels. In addition to dissolve control, this programmer can control tape recorders, lights, curtains, and other items as desired.

Picture courtesy Spindler and Sauppe.

called up and made part of the final effort. On the other hand, they can just as readily be erased if you choose not to use them.

A wide range of functions is available with programmers of this type. A homing command recycles the slide trays to "start" position, moving them clockwise or counter-clockwise, depending on the shortest distance. Various dissolve rates are provided, and the dissolve can be frozen at any point. Additionally, the dissolve phase is reversible, so that a particular slide can be partially dissolved and then pulled back up as many times as desired. Lamps can be turned off and the projector advanced, thus eliminating the need for blank slides. House lights of various kinds can be controlled in conjuction with live segments of a presentation, and zooms that are much like those that are achieved with motion picture cameras are possible. This is just a sample of the many capabilities of the sophisticated programmer; the list is far from complete, but it gives an idea of what is possible.

Of course, there is a problem with loss of memory if the power is cut, but this concern is easily dealt with by transferring all functions to tape for permanent storage.

Programming the presentation with the tone-control unit involves going through the cue script one line at a time while pressing the keys that correspond to the cues on the script. As you press the keys, a tone of a frequency that denotes a particular key, and thus a specific channel, is encoded onto the signal track of the tape. When the process is reversed, and the programmer is in the "play back" rather than the "record" mode, the presentation will run through automatically in exactly the same sequence in which it was programmed by hand.

But, what if you make a mistake and punch the wrong key? This is bound to happen—it is virtually impossible to get all the way through a presentation without making a mistake or two. No need to worry, though, for it is a simple task to

Figure 9

A six-projector set-up with a programmer/dissolve that features infinitely variable dissolve rates, animation, titling, superimposition, etc.

Picture courtesy Simon Associates.

back up and reprogram a segment. As with any tape recording, when a new signal is placed over a previously recorded portion, the old signal is erased and the new one encoded onto the tape. Eventually, with practice, the individual doing the programming should be able to proceed completely through the program with few mistakes. This is unimportant when the signals are being placed on tape, since corrections can be made easily. But, if a programmer is not available, and the presentation is being manually controlled by pressing remote advances, then this becomes a real concern. When this approach is used, as it may well be due to the lack of a programmer, practice is the key to achieving a satisfactory final effect. Manually-presented multi-image programs might at times incorporate a few functional errors, but the nature of the medium is such that an alert operator can quickly get back "in sync" without the audience ever having known that something was amiss.

To prepare for a manually-operated show, the remote units that control the individual projectors are lined up and taped to a table or a board. A patch of tape of a different color is attached to each of the units—use tape (or paint) that is maximally contrasty. The cue script has the cue spots colored also—the colors matching those on the remote advance units. As the operator (or operators) works through the script, he or she matches colors right on through to the final slide. With practice, the end result will be almost as smooth as the programmed version. There is a difference, however—the programmer, unlike its human counterpart, has no nerves and therefore suffers no anxiety as it methodically controls the presentation. So, here is a real advantage; once the signals are properly encoded onto the tape, everyone is able to sit back, relax, and enjoy the show, knowing full well that it will run the same way each and every time.

It should be mentioned that during the actual programming session, you should forget all about the slides. If you attempt to program with all of the equipment in place, the process, which should be rather routine, can get out of hand. For one thing, it is difficult to attend to everything at once, and you will find yourself watching the slides on the screen, and missing a cue or two. Then there is the noise of the cycling projectors, which can be quite distracting. It is suggested that you simply use the cue script, the programmer, and the recorder for this session, bringing the dissolve units and projectors on-line only when you plan a trial run to check out the complete presentation or selected segments of it.

This approach works best when a definite script is used. If your visuals are to be orchestrated to a musical accompaniment, you might find that it is easier to hit the key in concert with the screen image. This is a less structured approach and requires a few dry runs to develop a sense of how things should all come together.

There are different ways in which to code the cue script, but the most common approach involves the use of three basic devices. First, to indicate a visual on a specific screen, a simple sketch is drawn in the corresponding box on the script or storyboard. Then, to indicate a slide that is carried over (not changed), the word "hold" is written in the appropriate box. Finally, to identify a screen that will be black (no image), the word "black" is written in the appropriate box. An alternative to this approach is to use an arrow that points from the image box to the "hold" box, and to draw a cross through those boxes that indicate a black screen.

Also, you may find it useful to underline the key word in the narration that serves as the cue to change the slide. Additionally, when music is used rather than narration, you will have to indicate the specific point at which the slide should change by identifying the attendant musical effect, e.g., "clash of symbols," "sound of kettle drum," etc. (See Appendix A.)

Once the programming has been accomplished, you are ready to critically review the presentation with the objectives continually in mind. Hopefully, everything will sound and appear as you hoped that it would, but, if there are problems, now is the time to iron them out and develop the polish that is needed for the big event.

8.

Environmental Preparation

You will need some kind of facility in which to present the multi-image program, and, within the space, you will need to arrange projectors, seating, and screens in a way that will provide an optimal environment for the show.

The projector is of considerable importance. Little has been said about this piece of equipment to this point, so now is the time to consider factors relating not only to physical arrangement, but also to selection.

The Projectors

In actuality, the selection of this piece of equipment may well be a moot point, with the decisions having already been made earlier by someone else down the line. You will most likely be required to use those machines that are in stock and available at the media center, but, if you have a hand in selection, here are some tips that will be useful.

Select Kodak projectors for your show, and, if possible, choose those that have the auto-focus feature. As you probably know, various factors can cause a slide to appear out of focus, even though it is properly positioned and mounted. The auto-focus projector resolves this problem in an instant, thus maintaining a constant array of sharp images on the screens. A qualification must be added to this statement: the auto-focus feature is most desirable when slides are changed slowly, or when dissolves are used. If your slides are to change rapidly, you may not want the projectors to attempt a sharp focus after every slide change. If this is the case, then you may want to turn the focus switch to "off" position, thus bypassing this normally desirable feature. Another tip: have a spare projector handy in case a bulb burns out in one of your on-line machines. It is much simpler to switch machines than it is to try to change a lamp.

Kodak makes two distinct kinds of projectors, one for the popular market, and one for professionals. If you are able to do so, choose the Ektagraphic model. These give more accurate slide registration than does the "non-professional" Carousel model. The accurate slide registration feature becomes important when panoramas and dissolves based on exact slide-to-slide registration are being shown.

Ektagraphic projectors employ more sophisticated electronic components to control electromagnetic interference than does the simpler Carousel, and they are less prone to generate interference with tape players and programmers that manifests itself as an audible "pop." Ektagraphics also have larger, more powerful motors that run cooler and last longer.

Although projectors other than Kodak models might be used, it has been the experience of most teachers who have tried them that they tend to jam much more frequently than does the gravity-feed Kodak. If a slide is not in perfect alignment, it is still forced into position by the mechanical-feed models, often with disastrous results.

Let's talk about light sources. Many people believe that one projector of a given type is just like all others of that type, but this is not necessarily true. Different lamps in otherwise identical machines can make all the difference in the world when you project the images onto the screens.

If you have had much to do with school media equipment, you know that standardization is a problem. You are likely to get at least one lamp that is different from the rest, and there have been instances in which the three projector lamps all were different. The eye is an incredibly adaptable instrument. It tells us that daylight is white, when in fact it tends toward the blue. The eye tells us that the orange of the tungsten desk lamp is white, along with the light coming from the fluorescent fixture overhead. But when these different light sources are observed together, side by side on a surface, the eye no longer accepts them as being "just white"; rather, it tells us that here are several different colors of light. So, it is easy to see why matching light sources are so critical for a quality multi-image presentation. Images projected adjacent to one another are readily compared for various qualities, including hue equivalency.

The Projector Stands

Place your projectors in such a way that once they have been adjusted and focused, they will not be prone to movement. Wrapping the power cord around a table leg is one way to prevent the machine from being pulled off and damaged if someone should get tangled up in the cord. Use sturdy multiple projector stands if you can get them. Kodak publication S-55 describes a sturdy, two-projector stand called a "piggyback" that is useful where dissolves will be used. Other companies make stands of varying designs and prices; check the chapter on equipment sources for addresses.

You don't really need special stands, though; a table will do, or better still, two tables stacked one on top of the other. This arrangement can be a bit hazardous if the tables do not fit properly. Heavy tables are preferred, and a substantial overhang provides room for the legs of the upper table to be anchored on the lower one. You might use a single table, but the projectors will have to be steeply angled in order to project over the heads of the audience and onto the large screen surface. Such an angle can cause the slides in the 140 tray to bind up. Some producers insist on nothing larger than the 80-slide tray in order to avoid this problem.

Figure 10

Two projectors positioned on a projector stand with an attached dissolve unit. Such an arrangement is used for each screen of a multiple-screen presentation.

Picture courtesy Spindler and Sauppe.

The Screens

You will need some screens. A projection surface can be anything from a white wall to a panorama screen, with an entire array of options in between. Some educators use large sheets of butcher paper taped to the wall—an arrangement that is not ideal but which works quite well for school-produced shows. When standard single-slide screens are available, acquire three of these and line them up in a row—this makes an excellent projection arrangement.

Rear-view screens can also be used. Unlike those just mentioned, rear-view screens are translucent, and the image is projected from the back of the screen rather than from the front. This arrangement has the advantage of allowing the producer to position the equipment.

After the equipment has been set up, and the screens arranged, you should project some images to provide an idea

Figure 11

A multi-image projection screen arrangement. Shown here is a portable unit that is easily disassembled. White strips are available to cover the two black separators when panoramas are being projected.

Picture courtesy Da-Lite Screen Company.

Figure 12

A rear-projection screen. This is a lightweight, portable model. Several of these are combined for multi-image presentations.

Picture courtesy Impact Communications, Inc.

---

as to just what to expect relative to image size, position, etc. At this point, align the projectors. If you have dissolves and panoramas incorporated into the presentation, you will have to do some rather precise positioning to insure the correct registration of the multiple images at the specific point in time that they must all work together. If the facility is quite large, you may find that the lenses on the projectors are not up to the demands placed upon them by the long throw distance, and you will be forced to locate more suitable lenses.

Electrical Considerations

You should check the outlets in the facility to make certain there is a sufficient number to handle all of your pieces of equipment. Additionally, check the electrical set-up to determine how many outlets come from single breakers. If you have time, you can do this by flipping the breaker switch and then plugging in equipment to see if a given outlet is or is not hot. If you overload a circuit, the switch will open automatically, and there goes your show. Often, a custodian or maintenance person will know the details of the wiring plan and will share these with you. This certainly simplifies the process of getting acquainted with the power potential of the facility.

When you string your cords, place them under carpets or tape them down with wide strips of tape if they are in a place where there is a traffic flow.

Climate Control

Check for light leaks. Many facilities were not actually built to house projected presentations and, especially if it is during the day, light will creep in from everywhere. Be sure that you have plenty of tape. Often, small areas around windows can be caulked with this. You might even tape up pieces of cardboard or newspaper to block small leaks.

You probably won't be able to do much about the provisions for heating, cooling, and ventilation that have been built into the facility, but you can at least make maximum use of what is there. If it is cool outside, you might open windows to vent the room prior to the show. If the reverse is true, and it is hot outside, check the air conditioning, if available, for proper adjustment. Schools in many parts of the country lack the air conditioning feature. In cases such as these, it is best to keep the shades drawn in an effort to block as much external heat as possible. If you have time to do so, and the administration doesn't object, you can lower the internal temperature several degrees by taping aluminum foil to the windows. Such a surface reflects a great amount of heat, while black drapes, on the other hand, tend to absorb the heat. You will simply have to use common sense and hope for the best if the facility is new to you, realizing that few makeshift accommodations ever approach the ideal.

Seating

Finally, there is the seating consideration. If the facility that you will use has fixed seats, there is not much more to be said about the situation. However, if the seats are movable, you have some options. If seats are positioned too close to the screen (you can check this out yourself by actually sitting in a chair that is moved back and forth in relation to the screen), those individuals occupying the front rows will have difficulty dealing with the wide visual array. Additionally, if the screens are vertically extended, another viewing difficulty is introduced. You may find that a semi-circular arrangement works well, or try an arrangement in which the seats are clustered toward the center of the room (this works well for small groups). If an auditorium-type facility with tiered seats is available, visibility will be maximized. You can generally find such an arrangement in the school auditorium. Use this facility if at all possible, for it will resolve most of your seating and visibility problems in one stroke.

The Audience

Now that all is in readiness, your audience will shortly appear upon the scene. Have you presented them with a few preliminaries to get them set for what they are about to see? If not, they just might experience a bit of difficulty with the multi-image format. On the other hand, experienced groups probably need no technical introduction, but they shouldn't be thrown to the lions without at least being told, within limits, what the presentation is about. With a little practice, you will develop a sense for what is and what is not effective from the standpoint of audience preparation.

9.

Case Studies

Case Study One

One of the earlier and more successful attempts to merge the art of multi-image into the public school experience was conducted by Richard M. Glendening at Henry M. Gunn Senior High School in Palo Alto, California.

Built around a musical theme that included a selection of pieces ranging from classical works to hard rock, the program was calculated to evoke a broad range of emotional reactions from the audience.

Glendening used just about everything that he could lay his hands on for the hardware. The magnitude of the undertaking might be considered rather modest when compared to some of the 20 and 30 projector super shows of today, but given the public school setting and the pioneering nature of the project, it must be viewed with some degree of admiration and awe.

Included in the array of equipment were overhead projectors, slide projectors, motion picture projectors, and a tape recorder. The software selection was a potpourri of motion picture films (including a couple of time-lapse versions), available and locally-produced slides, and a creative touch which involved the use of trays filled with colored fluid which served as projectibles on the overheads. To pull all of this together and make it work, a team consisting of students

74

and teachers evolved. Like actors, each member of the team had to "come onstage" at the proper cue, and exit at precisely the right time. Such a synchronized effort obviously involved considerable teamwork and practice.

Students, parents, and staff members were impressed by the experience; an experience that transcended the barriers to communication that evolve from a complex, multi-faceted society such as ours.

Case Study Two

You are never too young to enjoy presentations based on the concept of multiple images. Ned Wert and Charles Battaglini, reporting on a series of presentations given to elementary children in Pennsylvania, emphasize the value of this approach in motivating young people.

The presentations were on a variety of subjects, and were open-ended in design so that they might be utilized with a broad range of audiences and in a variety of subject-matter areas. Among the media that were used were slides, Super-8 films, film loops, and audiotapes.

One presentation, with a circus theme, included an array of slides that were a mix of actual scenes from a circus along with pictures from a variety of books and magazines. Appropriate circus music accompanied the slides, and a circus "barker" furnished the narration.

The authors report:"The circus presentation has stimulated students toward creative responses in art, body movement, creative dramatics, social studies, music, and creative writing, as well as other areas of the curriculum."

An "underwater" presentation incorporated an even greater and more diverse selection of media. The creators of this program used slides and Super-8 films to project multiple images of fish that seemed to move around the room due to the technique of projecting the slides through a moving prism. "Bubbles" were reflected from a mirrored dome that rotated in front of a film loop projector.

This presentation was used in a variety of ways and with different grade levels. In the art class, it served to motivate the children in the areas of painting, printing, and sculpture. The music teacher used it in a silent mode, letting the students supply their own accompaniment. In other subject-matter areas, it served to introduce a vocabulary lesson, and to stimulate students to express themselves through body movement.

The authors report that there is strong evidence to indicate that the children who have been involved with the various programs have become more "visually literate," and have been highly motivated in various ways. Both students and teachers have become more sensitive to the conceptual and aesthetic requirements involved in creating such programs. Those involved in the planning and production aspects have realized a variety of positive spin-offs that relate to both cognitive and affective learning.

Wert and Battaglini are careful to use the term "multi-media" rather than the term "multi-image" in describing their programs. From the point of view of the purist, the programs do not quite conform to the definition of multi-image as currently accepted (see Introduction to this publication). If the discrepancy troubles you, keep in mind that few elementary schools actually have access to programmers that would handle presentations of the nature of those reported. Additionally, the three-screen format goes out the window when all available surfaces, including walls and ceiling, are used as "screens."

The two case studies cited above were reported originally in the pages of *Audiovisual Instruction* and of *Learning Resources*, published by AECT; see the Bibliography for complete information.

10.

Future Trends

Future trends tend to be more readily predicted for some media than for others. For example, a few years back, many experts were convinced that the Super-8 motion picture format would eventually supersede the 16mm format. That prediction was not borne out; in fact, both the Super-8 and the 16 have suffered at the hands of a relative newcomer, the videocassette. Now there is the videodisc for the soothsayers to ponder over. Best guesses suggest that it represents the imaging format of the future for educational applications, but, who knows for certain? At any rate, it is interesting to speculate about multi-image and what might occur in this field during the next few years.

It is tempting to predict that the revolution in programmers will continue at an exponential rate, especially when the amazing advances that have occurred in the recent past are considered. The evolutionary cycle from the early tone-control units up through punched-tape units and on to the highly sophisticated microprocessors has taken but a very few years, with advanced units being superseded by even more sophisticated ones almost before the ink has had a chance to dry on the literature. It appears, though, that we have about caught up with basic technology at this point in time.

The sophisticated multi-image programmer is a child of the

computer industry—a spin-off. Consequently, any startling breakthroughs in the basic design of programmers must await antecedent breakthroughs in computer design. There is little doubt that this will happen at some point in the future, but, for the present and for some time to come, programmers will probably not change radically in their basic structure and function. They will enjoy, however, a degree of refinement. Programmers will probably be less expensive and simpler to use, which means that they will become more available to educators. This in turn implies that multi-image presentations will most likely enjoy wider use throughout the educational realm.

A more manageable way in which to package and disseminate multi-image presentations is sorely needed. Today, most presentations are one-of-a-kind, and they typically reside in one location, living out their life there. Rather than going out to an audience, the audience comes to the medium—a marked contrast to the more traditional kinds of media, such as filmstrip and slide packages. The reason for this is obvious, of course. The logistics of dealing with the infinitely more complex multi-image presentation makes its widespread use very difficult. In the future, people who are skilled in packaging and marketing will devise ways in which many of these problems can be overcome, although, at this point in time, it is difficult to conceive of exactly how this will take place.

Current trends point to an increasing effort to research all aspects of communicating with multiple images. In the future, research findings will come together in the form of more concrete guidelines for conceiving, creating, and utilizing the multi-image medium. To date, information is rather scanty, and it is spread throughout the literature. Tomorrow, however, the situation will be different. More and more bright doctoral students are looking at perception, mental imagery, "visual literacy," communication theory, etc., as rich areas in which to write dissertations. Educators as a group are becoming more aware of all aspects of visual communication, a trend that has no doubt been facilitated by such entertainment media as television, film spectaculars, and, yes, multi-image.

The future result of this burgeoning interest in multi-image will be a knowledge pool from which all can draw according to their needs.

11.

Student Projects

1. *Present a Live Multi-Image Presentation.* This is an excellent way in which to introduce the medium. Ask for three volunteers from your class. Tell them that they will act out the moods of a musical selection, each student to interpret the music in his or her own personal way. Rig up three directional light sources (can be projectors). The effect is best if a different colored gel is placed over each of the three lights. Position the students at three stations across the front of the room—they should be far enough apart so that they do not interfere with each other's movements, but close enough together to affect a certain overall unity. A plain, uncluttered background is best, but do the best that you are able where this is concerned. Turn the colored lights on, illuminating each of your three "images" with a different source. Turn off the room lights. Now, if you can settle the class down (they will be excited and expectant at this point), turn on the music and make it loud. If the talent is "programmed" properly, you will have a live multi-image presentation right in your own classroom.

2. *Compose Visible Music.* Have the students choose a musical selection that has a lot of "color." Or, use segments from a number of different selections that reflect different moods or feelings. Dub the segments onto a single tape. Play the tape through as many times as necessary to stimulate the

students to start thinking in terms of appropriate visual images for each part of the music. Stop the tape as needed so that ideas can be jotted down. Now, have the students locate pictures that coincide with the information that they wrote down on the "Storyboard." Photograph the pictures onto slides, tray them into two or three trays, and prepare for the show. It will take a bit of practice to keep the pictures synchronized with the music if you lack a programmer and must punch the remote advance keys by hand, but it doesn't make too much difference if the audio and visual components aren't exactly matched, because much more latitude is generally provided by a strictly musical accompaniment than by a narration. However, there may be points in the presentation where the visual should precisely match the audio.

3. *Create Multi-Image Art.* With your class, locate an interesting story, or write a new one. Assign different story segments to groups of three students for each segment. Physically separate the members of each team so that their drawings will be original and will not be influenced by the work of other team members. Have each team member interpret his or her segment graphically (the more colorful, the better) on a sheet that has a ratio of two units to three. The idea is to develop three different interpretations of a single idea. The total number of pictures will depend on the length of the story that is being used as the basis for the presentation. Using slide film, photograph the pictures. Place the finished slides in sets of three into Carousel trays, one member of the set in each tray. Each set of three slides will come from a given team, and will illustrate a given segment of the story. Narrate the story onto a tape, or simply read it as the slides are shown. A bit of music adds atmosphere. Perhaps you might play a record or a tape of an appropriate selection in the background. Hand the remote advance from each projector to a different student, telling all to stay "in sync" the best that they can. Turn on the equipment.

The learning that takes place in this activity relates to several important requisites of multi-image. First, the development of mental images from information that has been encoded in a different format stimulates the students to "think visually." Second, the creation of the illustrations constitutes an additional exercise in visualizing ideas, but this time the image can be shared by all. Third, a photographic exercise is included. Even though the students might do nothing more than look through the viewfinder and click the shutter at this point, for many it will be their very first exposure to a copy camera. Fourth, the students will have an experience with the traying of slides; a modest experience to be sure, but they will learn that slides must be placed in the trays in a certain way. Fifth, they will learn (at times the hard way) about the importance of maintaining all aspects of the presentation "in sync," and they will come to value the importance of some kind of programming plan or device that will insure a smooth presentation.

4. *Make a Multi-Image Storyboard.* Collectively, you and your class should develop some kind of theme, brainstorming together until a rough script falls into place. Assign separate sheets containing the skeleton script, but no pictures, to individuals or small groups. Instruct them to fill in the blank rectangles with sketches that they perceive as being appropriate to accompany the script. Now, place the total script together, in sequence, and critique it, making modifications where transitions seem ragged. This activity should be a precursor to subsequent steps in the development of a finished production.

5. *Write a Multi-Image Script.* Although many individuals like the storyboard approach just described, and use it consistently, there are those who find it too confining. These folks often find it easier to write a script that is accompanied by a general description of appropriate visuals. To use this technique, you should first write a polished script in one

column of a two-column format. In the second column, and adjacent to the appropriate verbal material, indicate in general terms what you think the attendant visuals should look like. Now, start your search. Assign students to look for pictures that fall into general kinds of categories. For example, if one segment of your presentation deals with environmental concerns, students might select from a vast array of pictures in current magazines those examples that they deem to be particularly effective. A rather large pool of pictures will rapidly accumulate, and you will have no difficulty in illustrating the ideas that are spelled out in your script.

6. *Make Some Titles.* Purchase some Kodalith film and developer. Run through your storyboard or script and identify all of the frames that involve lettering of some kind. Let the students select from the list of captions those that each would like to make. Using markers, speedball pens, cut-out letters, or other lettering techniques, the students should form the captions on white cards that have a ratio of 2:3. Now, photograph the captions onto the Kodalith film. Mix the chemicals and let your students process the film under a red light source. Obtain some dye (food coloring works, so do felt markers, but dye colors work best) and add color to your negative slides. Use opaque solution to block unwanted white areas, then mount the slides and include them along with the rest of the slides in your program. This is an effective technique which results in striking colored images against a solid black background.

7. *Program a Multi-Image Presentation.* If you have access to a programmer, this is a highly motivating activity for students. You will need to have a script or storyboard of some kind, even though the audio portion of the presentation is strictly musical. With a musical accompaniment, the script will contain fewer specific instructions, as a rule, and the approach to programming will be more of a trial-and-error effort than would be the case with a narrated script.

If you do have a programmer, it will most likely be one of the tone-control varieties. These are fine for young students, because all that they require is that the correct key be pressed at the right time. Although it is not the custom to do so, you might have the projectors functioning during the programming sequence just so that the students can experience the excitement of the whole thing. There is a problem with this approach, however; the person involved in programming often becomes so caught up with the visuals that he or she forgets to press the key on cue. Of course, all that is required to correct this problem is to re-record the signal so that it is in the right place.

8. *Put on a Multi-Image Show.* Once all of the make-ready has taken place and the titles are made, slides placed in trays, tapes dubbed, programming completed, etc., your students are ready for the big event—the actual presentation of their multi-image show. You will find that with a modicum of assistance, they will be more than competent in handling this responsibility. And what heroes and heroines they will be in the eyes of the others in the school who see and enjoy the show! This is an excellent way in which to build youngsters' self-esteem.

12.

Glossary

Cue script. The outline of the multi-image program that contains some kind of key or directions that indicate the points at which signals are to be encoded by the programmer.

Cut. This term is used to describe the situation in which the light from one projector is cut off as that from the second one comes on.

Dissolve. A technique that uses two projectors, generally superimposed over the same screen area. The first scene is gradually diminished in intensity, while the second one increases. The effect is achieved through the selective control of light.

Drop-out. Also referred to as a "burn-in." A slide consisting of a transparent image on an opaque ground is projected over a positive image on the screen to achieve the effect of a white or colored overlay. Generally used for titling. When the negative line slide and the positive slide are combined together as a single slide through the use of a slide duplicator, the effect is a drop-out title on an image of some kind. This effect is achieved through the use of double-exposures.

Dupe. Short for "duplication," or "duplicate." Generally used to describe a second-generation slide that has been copied from an original.

Fade-in. Starting with the darkened screen, the image is slowly brought up to full intensity.

Fade-out. The opposite of fade-in. The image is at full intensity on the screen and is gradually diminished in intensity until the screen is black.

Fast cut. A technique in which the light from the projector is rapidly blocked, thus cutting off the image from the screen instantaneously.

Mixer. A device that permits sounds from several sources to be combined. More sophisticated mixers permit the operator to be highly selective in the manner in which this takes place.

Montage. A combination of elements from a number of different sources. Generally a term used in the fine arts.

Panorama. An integrated view across all or several screens. Typically involves a continuous scene.

Panorama head. An adjustable attachment that fits onto a tripod. This device permits the camera to be moved to three pre-determined positions. The three resulting slides (one taken at each position) will be so related that they can be projected onto the screens to duplicate the panorama view.

Real time. When certain kinds of programmers (tone-control) are used, it is necessary to place the signals onto the tape in the same time-span that it will subsequently take to play the presentation automatically. The time that it takes to accomplish this is referred to as "real time."

Storyboard. Cards or papers that contain a diagram which corresponds to the screens of the multi-image show are called storyboards. Visual and verbal notes are made in appropriate sections on the sheets or cards as planning evolves. The storyboard often serves as the basis for the cue script.

Sync. Short for synchronization. When visuals and audio are in perfect correspondence during playback, the program is said to be "in sync." With motion pictures, lip sync is the most difficult type of synchronization to handle. Where traditional slide presentations are concerned, the problem is generally not so acute, but with multi-image presentations, the synchronization between sounds and special effects can be extremely critical.

13.

Equipment Manufacturers and Distributors

AIC Photo, Inc., Carle Place, NY 11514 (Miranda cameras and accessories)

Ampex, 401 Broadway, Redwood City, CA 94063 (tape recorders)

Audio Visual Laboratories, Inc., 500 Hillside Avenue, Atlantic Highlands, NJ 07716 (multi-image computer system with programming and editing features)

Audiotronics, P.O. Box 3997, North Hollywood, CA 91609 (record players, tape recorders, dissolve units)

AV Technologies, Inc., P.O. Box 10583, Dallas, TX 75201 (projector stands)

Bell and Howell/Mamiya Company, 7100 McCormick Road, Chicago, IL 60645 (Mamiya cameras and accessories, tape recording equipment)

Berkey Marketing Companies, Inc., Kowa Camera Division, P.O. Box 1102, Woodside, NY 11377 (Kowa cameras)

Bogen Photo Corp., 100 South Van Brunt Street, P.O. Box 448, Englewood, NJ 07631 (Bowens Illumitran slide duplicator)

Buhl Optical, 1009 Beech Avenue, Pittsburgh, PA 15233 (stacking dissolve rack for Carousel projectors)

Canon U.S.A., Inc., 10 Nevada Drive, Lake Success, NY 11040 (cameras, lights, lenses)

Clear Light Projections, P.O. Box 391, Newton, MA 02158 (programmers and dissolve units)

Columbia Scientific Industries, P.O. Box 9908, Austin, TX 78766 (programmers, dissolve units, projector stands)

Commercial Picture Equipment, 5725 North Broadway, Chicago, IL 60660 (screens)

Da-Lite Screen, 3100 State Road 15N, Warsaw, IN 46580 (screens, projection stands)

Eastman Kodak Company, 343 State Street, Rochester, NY 14650 (Carousel projectors, dissolve units, cameras)

Electrosonic Systems, Inc., 5223 Edina Industrial Boulevard, Minneapolis, MN 55435 (dissolve units, programmers)

Entre Electronics, Beaverton, OR. Distributor: Simon Associates, 1019 Trillium Lane, Mill Valley, CA 94941 (programmers, dissolve units)

Hervic Corporation, 14225 Ventura Blvd., Sherman Oaks, CA 91423 (Topcon cameras)

Honeywell Photographic, P.O. Box 22083, Dept. No. 203-883, Denver, CO 80222 (Pentax cameras, Repronar slide duplicator)

Impact Communications, Inc., 9202 Markville Drive, Dallas, TX 75243 (slide production systems, slide duplicators, rear projection screen, dissolve units)

Konica Camera, P.O.Box 1102, Woodside, NY 11377 (cameras)

Light Impressions Corporation, P.O. Box 3012, Rochester, NY 14614 (slide viewers and sorters)

Lion Photo Supply, Inc., 4301 Fifth Ave., Aurora, IL 60505 (cameras of all makes, accessories, lenses, lights, screens)

Mackenzie Labs, 5507 Peck Road, Arcadia, CA 91006 (audio programmers, dissolve units, projector stands)

Maximilian Kerr Assoc., Inc., "Slidemagic System," 2040 Highway 35, Wall, NJ 07719 (pin-register 35mm multi-image camera)

Minolta Corporation, 101 Williams Drive, Ramsey, NJ 07446 (cameras)

Nikon, Inc., Dept. N-42, Garden City, NY 11530 (Nikon cameras, Nikkor panorama head)

Ponder and Best, Inc., 1630 Stewart Street, Santa Monica, CA 90406 (Olympus cameras, Vivitar lighting equipment and lenses)

Radmar, Inc., 1282 Old Skokie Road, Highland Park, IL 60035 (slide duplicators)

Simon Associates, 1019 Trillium Lane, Mill Valley, CA 94941 (Entre programmer and dissolve units)

Slik Division, Berkey Marketing Companies, P.O. Box 1102, Woodside, NY 11377; 1011 Chestnut Street, Burbank, CA 91506 (tripods with panorama guide)

Smith-Victor Sales Corporation, 301 North Colfax Street, Griffith, IN 46319 (tripods with 3-way panorama heads)

Sony Corporation of America, 9 West 57th Street, New York, NY 10019 (tape recorders)

Spindler and Sauppe, 13034 Saticoy Street, North Hollywood, CA 91605 (dissolve controls, magnetic tape, programmers, punched-tape programmers, electronic microprocessors, projector stackers, all types of accessories)

Spiratone, Inc., 135-06 Northern Blvd., Flushing, NY 11354 (special filters and lenses, slide copying equipment, programmers, dissolve units)

3M Company, 3M Center, P.O. Box 33600, Saint Paul, MN 55133 (screens, dissolve units, microprocessor programmers, stereo visual sync recorders, etc.)

Tiffen Manufacturing Company, 90 Oser Avenue, Hauppauge, NY 11787 (projector stands, programmers, dissolve units)

Yashica, Inc., 411 Sette Drive, Paramus, NJ 07652 (cameras, lenses, tripods)

14.

Materials Manufacturers and Distributors

Ampex, 401 Broadway, Redwood City, CA 94063 (audio tapes)

Artype, Inc., 345 East Terra Cotta Ave., Crystal Lake, II 60014 (pressure-sensitive letters)

Beckley-Cardy Co., 1900 North Narragansett, Chicago, IL 60639 (drawing and lettering supplies)

Dick Blick, P.O. Box 1267, Galesburg, IL 61401 (graphic art materials)

Bourges Color Corp., 80 Fifth Ave., New York, NY 10017 (self-adhering film for graphics)

Braun North American, 55 Cambridge Parkway, Cambridge, MA 02142 (slide mounts)

Chart-Pak Rotex, 4 River Road, Leeds, MA 01053 (pressure-sensitive letters)

Craftint Mfg. Co., 1850 Euclid Ave., Cleveland, OH 44112 (graphic art materials)

Dennison Manufacturing Co., Farmingham, MA 01702 (cut-out letters)

Eastman Kodak Company, 343 State Street, Rochester, NY 14650 (films, filters, slide mounts, etc.)

Edmund Scientific Company, Dept. EL, 20 Edscorp Building, Barrington, NJ 08007 (colored filters of various kinds)

Ed-Tech Service Company, P.O. Box 407, Chatham, NJ 07928 (film markers, slide mounts, blank slide film for handmade slides, lettering)

Erie Color Slide Club, Inc., P.O. Box 672, Erie, PA 16512 (slide masks for use between cover glass, pressure-sensitive cardboard mounts, heat-seal mounts)

Higgins Ink Co., Inc., 271 Ninth Street, Brooklyn, NY 11215 (graphic art materials)

W.W. Holes Manufacturing Company, St. Cloud, MN 56301 (cut-out letters)

Hunt Speedball, 1405 Locust Street, Philadelphia, PA 19102 (inks, pens, watercolors)

Instantype, Inc., 7005 Tujanga Avenue, North Hollywood, CA 91605 (ready-made lettering)

Koh-I-Noor, Inc., 100 North Street, Bloomsbury, NJ 08804 (pens, inks)

Letraset, Inc., 2379 Charles Road, Mountain View, CA 94040 (pressure-sensitive letters)

Lion Photo Supply, Inc., 4301 Fifth Ave., Aurora, IL 60505 (multi-image filters, bulk slide film)

Salis International, 4040 North 29th Ave., Hollywood, FL 33020 (P.H. Martin's watercolor dyes)

Sanford Ink Company, 2740 Washington Blvd., Bellwood, IL 60104 (graphic art materials)

Spiratone, Inc., 135-06 Northern Blvd., Flushing, NY 11354 (mounts, filters, lenses, matte boxes for slide effects)

Stik-A-Letter Company, Route 2, Box 1400, Escondido, CA 92025 (cut-out lettering)

Redikut Letter Company, 12617 South Prairie Avenue, Hawthorne, CA 90250 (3-D letters)

20th Century Plastics, Inc., 3629 Crenshaw Blvd., Los Angeles, CA 90016 (plastic organizers, pages and albums for slide storage)

Visual Horizons, 209 Westfall Rd., Rochester, NY 14520 (high-contrast slide masks)

Volk Corporation, Box 72, Pleasantville, NJ 08232 (clip art)

Wess Plastic Company, 50 Schmitt Boulevard, Farmingdale, NY 11735 (pin-register glass and glassless slide mounts, slide blanks, slide mount accessories)

Winsor and Newton, Inc., 555 Winsor Drive, Secaucus, NJ 07094 (designer's colors)

Bibliography

Anderson, J.A. Single-Channel and Multi-Channel Messages: A Comparison of Connotative Meaning. *Audio Visual Communication Review,* 1969, 17, 428-434.

Audiovisual Notes from Kodak: "A Preshow Checklist for Effective Dissolve Projection." Publication No. S-14. Rochester, NY: Eastman Kodak Co., 1978.

Audiovisual Notes from Kodak: "How to Get into Motion." Periodical No. T-91-8-2. Rochester, NY: Eastman Kodak Co., 1978.

Audiovisual Notes from Kodak: "Multi-Image." Periodical No. T-91-9-1. Rochester, NY: Eastman Kodak Co., 1979.

Baker, E.L., and Popham, W.J. *Expanding Dimensions of Instructional Objectives.* Englewood Cliffs, NJ: Prentice-Hall, Inc., 1973.

Balsey, G. Planning Multimedia Production. *Photomethods,* 1976, 19(5), 34,36.

Beckman, C.J. Producing Multi-Image: Getting Started Part 1. *Audiovisual Instruction,* 1977, 22(3), 70-74.

Beckman, C.J. Producing Multi-Image: Getting Started Part 2. *Audiovisual Instruction,* 1977, 22(4), 53-55.

Beckman, C.J. Producing Multi-Image: Getting Started Part 3. *Audiovisual Instruction,* 1977, 22(5), 53-54.

Benedict, J.A., and Crane, D.A. *Producing Multi-Image Presentations.* Tempe, AZ: Arizona State University, 1973.

Bloom, B. (Ed.) *Taxonomy of Educational Objectives, Handbook I: Cognitive Domain.* New York, NY: David McKay, 1956.

Broadbent, D.E. *Perception and Communication.* New York, NY: Pergamon Press, 1958.

Brown, R.M. *Educational Media: A Competency-Based Approach.* Columbus, OH: Charles E. Merrill Publishing Co., 1973.

Bullough, R.V. *Creating Instructional Materials, 2nd ed.* Columbus, OH: Charles E. Merrill Publishing Co., 1978.

Gardner, C.H. How Educational Administrators View the P.R. Potential of Multi-Image. *Audiovisual Instruction,* 1977, 22(2), 18-19, 63.

Glendening, R.M. A Multimedia Educational Experience. *Audiovisual Instruction,* 1969, 14(4), 66-67.

Goldstein, E.B. The Perception of Multiple Images. *Audio-Visual Communication Review,* 1975, 23,34-68.

Gordon, R.L. (Ed.) *The Art of Multi-Image.* Abington, PA: Association for Multi-Image, 1978.

Hall, N. Your Program Syncs. *Audiovisual Instruction,* 1975, 20(9), 42-45.

Hershenson, M. Color in Your Darkroom. *Modern Photography,* 1979, 43(10), 42+.

Hill, H. Communication Research and Instructional Technology. *Educational Communication and Technology Journal,* 1978, 25, 47-54.

Hsia, H.J. The Information Processing Capacity of Modality and Channel Performance. *Audio Visual Communication Review,* 1971, 19, 51-75.

Hsia, H.J. Redundancy: Is It the Lost Key to Better Communication? *Audio Visual Communication Review,* 1977, 25, 63-85.

Hyzer, J. Making Simple, Effective Title and Graphic Slides. *Photomethods,* 1979, 22(10), 25-27, 79.

Instructional Design Series. Provo, UT: Courseware, Inc., 1974.

Kemp, J.E. *Planning and Producing Audiovisual Materials, 3rd ed.* New York, NY: Thomas Y. Crowell, 1975.

Kenny, M.F., and Schmitt, R.F. *Images, Images, Images.* Rochester, NY: Eastman Kodak Co., 1979.

Kodak Projector Feature Summary—A Guide to Kodak Professional Audiovisual Projectors. Publication No. S-5. Rochester, NY: Eastman Kodak Co., 1978.

Krathwohl, D.R. (Ed.) *Taxonomy of Educational Objectives, Handbook II: Affective Domain.* New York, NY: David McKay, 1964.

Kuo, F.F. Creating Visuals for a Multi-Screen Presentation. *Audiovisual Instruction,* 1972, 17(7), 83-85.

Langer, S.K. *Philosophy in a New Key.* Cambridge, MA: Harvard University Press, 1942.

Langford, M.J. *Visual Aids and Photography in Education.* New York, NY: Hastings House, 1973.

Lawson, B.R. Motivating with Multi-Image at the U.S. Military Academy: The Medium for the 70s and its Public Relations Side Benefits. *Audiovisual Instruction,* 1971, 16(5), 54-59.

Lukas, T.G. An Inexpensive, Easy to Build Slide-Tape Programmer. *Audiovisual Instruction,* 1975, 20(9), 46-58.

Lukas, T.G., Olsen, R.W., and Nisbet, J.J. Design an Automated 4 Slide, 2 Screen Projector System. *Learning Resources,* 1973, 18(7), 4-6.

Mager, R.F. *Preparing Instructional Objectives.* Palo Alto, CA: Fearon Publishers, 1962.

Mindell, M.I. Sound Synchronized Still Picture Programs. *Audiovisual Instruction,* 1976, 21(1), 57-59.

Nelson, M.R. The Art and Technique of Multimedia. *Audiovisual Instruction,* 1976, 21(8), 38-42.

Nibeck, R.G. Which Medium for the Future? *Audiovisual Instruction,* 1976, 21(1), 12-13, 71.

Perrin, D.G. A Theory of Multiple-Image Communication. *Audio Visual Communication Review,* 1969, 17, 368-382.

Piggyback Stand for Two-Screen or Dissolve Projection with Two Kodak Slide Projectors. Publication No. S-55. Rochester, NY: Eastman Kodak Co., 1977.

Randhawa, B.S., and Coffman, W.E. (Eds.) *Visual Learning, Thinking, and Communication.* New York, NY: Academic Press, 1978.

Rankowski, C.A., and Galey, M. Effectiveness of Multimedia in Teaching Descriptive Geometry. *Educational Communication and Technology Journal,* 1979, 27, 114-120.

Reflections on Professionalism: Some Questions and Answers About the Image Pit. Publication No. S-15-90-AP. Rochester, NY: Eastman Kodak Co., 1979.

Rock, I. *An Introduction to Perception.* New York: Macmillan, Inc., 1975.

Ryan, M. Preparing a Slide-Tape Program: A Step-by-Step Approach, Part I. *Audiovisual Instruction,* 1975, 20(7), 36-38.

Ryan, M. Preparing a Slide-Tape Program: A Step-by-Step Approach, Part II. *Audiovisual Instruction,* 1975, 20(9), 36-39.

Severin, W. Another Look at Cue Summation. *Audio-Visual Communication Review,* 1967, 15, 233-245.

Sleeman, P.J., Cobun, T.C., and Rockwell, D.M. *Instructional Media and Technology.* New York, NY: Longman, 1979.

Smith, M.D., Schagrin, M., and Poorman, L.E. Multimedia Systems: A Review and Report of a Pilot Project. *AudioVisual Communication Review,* 1967, 15, 345-369.

Stecker, E.E. Music on Cue. *Photomethods,* 1979, 22(10), 32-33+.

Swenson, M. Audio for Photographers. *Photomethods,* 1979, 22(11), 38-40.

Travers, R.M.W. *et al. Research and Theory Related to Audiovisual Information Transmission.* Washington, DC: U.S. Dept. of Health, Education, and Welfare, 1967.

Trohanis, P.L. Environmental Ecological Education via Simultaneously Projected Multiple-Images with Sound. *Audiovisual Instruction,* 1971, 16(1), 19-26.

Trohanis, P.L. Information Learning and Retention with

Multiple-Images and Audio. *Audio Visual Communication Review*, 1975, 23, 395-414.

Vento, C.J. Creative Experimental and Total Environmental Immersion. *Audiovisual Instruction*, 1970, 15(6), 48-49.

Wallington, J., Hale, P., and Conte, J. Multi-Image Festival. *Audiovisual Instruction*, 1969, 14(6), 53-54.

Wert, N.O., and Battaglini, C. Multi-Media: Motivation for the Arts and Basic Education. *Learning Resources*, 1975, 2(2), 21-22.

Wide-Screen and Multiple-Screen Presentations. Publication No. S028. Rochester, NY: Eastman Kodak Co., 1976.

Williams, D.J., and Jorgensen, E.S. The World of Multi-Image. *Audiovisual Instruction*, 1970, 15(6), 50-51.

Womeldorf, H.J. Photomurals an Effective Exhibit Tool. *Photomethods*, 1979, 22(10), 63-65, 70.

Annotated List of Media on Multi-Image

Basic Art Techniques for Slide Production. 55 color slides with script and tape narration. Eastman Kodak Co., Rochester, NY. An outline of basic techniques for preparing simple art work. Covers reasons for standardizing outside dimensions and working area of art work; describes various lettering systems, legibility standards, and useful materials for art work preparation.

Basic Copying. 77 slides with script and tape narration. Eastman Kodak Co., Rochester, NY. How to select equipment for a copy stand set-up and obtain good visual results from flat copy. Describes techniques of using a single-lens reflex camera; discusses selection of a copy stand, choice of film and close-up lenses, positioning of lights, and use of exposure meters.

Effective Visual Presentations. 16mm/Super-8 sound motion picture. Eastman Kodak Co., Rochester, NY. Discusses planning of a visual program, including defining of objectives, analyzing the audience, and selecting and organizing the content with the aid of a planning board. Covers production, including basic art and copying techniques. Gives suggestions for presenting an effective audiovisual program.

Frank Film. 16mm motion picture, sound and color. Pyramid

Films, Santa Monica, CA. Describes various phases of growing up in America through the filming of a multitude of images in collage form. Each collage is an endless swelling, growing, and shifting flood depicting the continuity of one's stream of consciousness. Multiple images change in rapid sequence with an attendant double sound track.

High Contrast Photography for Instruction. 16mm motion picture, sound, black and white or color. Indiana University, Bloomington, IN. Emphasizes the use of high contrast line film for the production of negatives and prints. Also covers several specialized techniques.

How to Prepare a Multimedia Storyboard. Manual and slides. 3M Company, Saint Paul, MN. An instructional manual complete with numerous examples of storyboards and a set of slides, which are arranged in a plastic album page for easy viewing. Shows how to set up projectors and screens, and shows in a step-by-step sequence how to prepare the storyboard.

Photographic Slides for Instruction. 16mm motion picture, sound, black and white or color. Indiana University, Bloomington, IN. Demonstrates the basic techniques for making photographic slides and explains their instructional purpose by showing a variety of uses. Includes the preparation and use of 2" x 2" color slides, simple copy work, and sound/slide presentation.

Producing a Sound/Slide Program. Slides with script and tape narration. Media Systems, Salt Lake City, UT. The basic techniques involved in producing a sound/slide program are covered in three segments, including planning, scripting, and recording (71 frames), graphics (76 frames), and photography (67 frames). Three filmstrips, three cassettes, and a teacher's guide.

Production Techniques for Instructional Graphic Materials. Slides/filmstrip with student manual, instructor's manual, audio-tutorial cassettes. Charles E. Merrill Publishing Co., Columbus, OH. Covers the basic techniques for photographing graphic materials onto the high contrast format; processing and uses of high contrast materials.

Sound: Recording and Reproduction. Six sound filmstrips, six audiocassettes with audible and inaudible advance signals, instructional manual. Media Systems, Salt Lake City, UT. Topics covered include record players and turntables, amplifiers and audio systems, microphones and speakers, mixing and editing, tape recorders, recording, and reproduction.

Synchronizing a Slide/Tape Program. 66 slides with script and tape narration. Eastman Kodak Co., Rochester, NY. Covers procedure for synchronizing slides with an audiotape, including step-by-step instructions for recording cues. Discusses the advantages of a synchronized sound-slide program.

Thinking Photographically. 80 slides, taped narration. Media Loft, Inc., Minneapolis, MN. Based on a practical approach to solving compositional problems in photography.

Utilizing the Tape Recorder. Sound filmstrip. Media Systems, Salt Lake City, UT. Covers the use of the tape recorder with emphasis on school applications. Sections on the mechanics of tape recording, steps in tape recording, and uses of recordings.

Appendix A

Scripts and Storyboards

	1	2	3
1 2 3			
☐☐☐ —			
☐☐☐ —			
☐☐☐ —			
☐☐☐ —			
☐☐☐ —			
☐☐☐ —			
☐☐☐ —			

page____   project_____

Here is a useful storyboard-script. This format can be adapted to most of the three-screen presentations that would be produced in the schools.

1 2 3		1	2	3
□□□ 1	(Introductory music)	BLACK	BLACK	BLACK
□☒□ 2	(Introductory music)	HOLD	[skier]	HOLD
□☒□ 3	(music fades) Crystal air, the scent of balsam fir, two feet of fresh powder, the challenge of the slope, exhilaration-- that's skiing.	HOLD	[trail]	HOLD
☒☒☒ 4	But, in order to enjoy it all, you must know the rules of the slopes, and that's skiing safety.	THAT'S SKIING	SAFE	[mountains]
☒☒☒ 5	Let's meet Rick. He's a member of the National Ski Patrol, and he'll be our host for this program.	[Rick]	BLACK	BLACK
□☒□ 6	He's going to acquaint us with the various signs that are used to give the condition of a particular run.	HOLD	[sign]	HOLD
□□☒ 7	He'll also tell us what to do if we should encounter an injured skier.	HOLD	HOLD	[injured skier]

page 1   project *That's Skiing Safety*

A finished multi-image storyboard-script. Note the cue column to the left of the sheet; it is composed of three small squares or boxes that represent the keys on the programmer. The numbers 1, 2, 3, etc., under the cue boxes are the frame numbers; they correspond to the first set of images to be seen on the screen, the second set, etc. The X in the box indicates that the person doing the programming should press the key on the programmer that corresponds to the specific box. So, on frame 4, for example, all of the keys would be pressed to change all slides. The same is true for frame 5, but in frame 6 only one slide, the middle one, is changed. When blank slides are used, the term "black" is indicated in the image boxes to the right of the sheet; when a slide is held from one sequence to the next, the term "hold" is used.

106

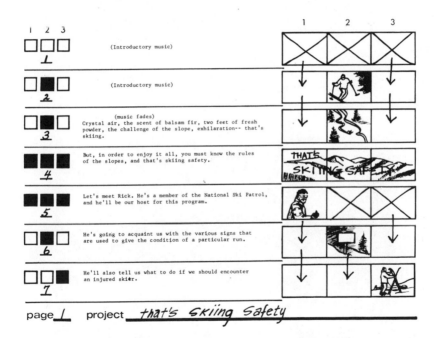

	1	2	3

(Introductory music)

1

(Introductory music)

2

(music fades)
Crystal air, the scent of balsam fir, two feet of fresh powder, the challenge of the slope, exhilaration-- that's skiing.

3

But, in order to enjoy it all, you must know the rules of the slopes, and that's skiing safety.

4

Let's meet Rick. He's a member of the National Ski Patrol, and he'll be our host for this program.

5

He's going to acquaint us with the various signs that are used to give the condition of a particular run.

6

He'll also tell us what to do if we should encounter an injured skier.

7

page *1* project *that's skiing safety*

This storyboard is like the one shown in the previous plate, but a slightly different code has been used. The cue boxes to the left are filled in solidly, or, you may wish to use a color code. The image boxes to the right use crosses through the boxes to indicate a black screen, while arrows are used to indicate a "hold."

Programming a presentation with the tone-control programmer. Note the stacked projectors, the dissolve units, and the stereo recorder. The keys on the programmer are pressed according to the code that is indicated in the cue column on the storyboard.

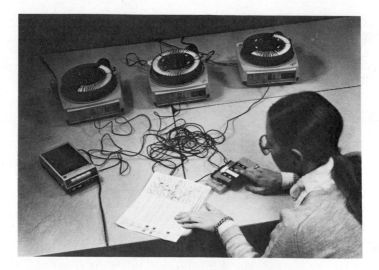

Operating a manually-controlled, multi-image set-up. The three remotes are attached to a board for easy access. Each is coded with a different color which matches the colors in the cue boxes on the storyboard.

AUDIO	VISUAL
(Introductory Music) (Music gradually increases in volume, cadence changes from "snow music" to "racing music.") (Cacophony of loud sounds— then, abrupt silence.) Now what! There lies your friend in the snow; she's hurt, she needs help, and the next move is yours.	Screens are black, panorama view of Powder Mountain ski area fades in to fill all screens. Screens are filled in rapid succession by different views of skiers in action. Alternate screens randomly, until 15-20 slides are shown. Screens two and three abruptly black. Screen one shows injured skier. Hold on screen one for six seconds. Beginning with screen two, pop on successively closer views of injured skier until ECU of face is shown. Hold on this.

A multi-image script. This is an optional format that is useful when the complexity of the presentation makes it cumbersome to use the more traditional three-block format.

Title: **Plan Sheet**   BY:

Objective: DATE

Audience   PAGE

Narrative	CUE	Channels			Channel Content
		1	2	3	

This storyboard-script format can be used for a number of different applications including multi-image.

From *INSTRUCTIONAL MEDIA AND TECHNOLOGY: A Guide to Accountable Learning Systems,* by Phillip J. Sleeman, Ted C. Cobun, and D.M. Rockwell. Copyright © 1979 by Longman, Inc. Reprinted with permission of Longman.

Appendix B

Inexpensive Equipment

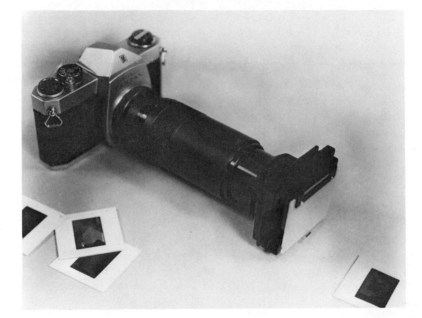

An inexpensive slide copier that attaches to the 35mm camera. The normal lens is removed from the camera, and the copier attached in its place. At the forward end of the device is the slide holder, which has a spring-loaded "gate" that holds the slide securely in position. A piece of frosted glass diffuses the light so that even illumination is obtained. By pointing the camera at a strong light source, sufficient illumination can be obtained to make it possible to make excellent copies of existing slides at a modest cost. By double exposing a slide, it is also possible to make composite titles of various kinds.

A homemade copy stand. To obtain plans for this stand, write to Eastman Kodak Company and ask for publication T-43; there is a modest charge for this publication. The stand that is illustrated was made from inexpensive particle board. Bolts and wing nuts were used throughout so that it might be disassembled and stored, or transported with ease.

An inexpensive, battery-operated sound mixer. The three dials on the front of this unit are used to control the volume of the inputs from three separate sound sources. On the back are three inputs that permit the sound to be fed from the various sources into the unit. There is an output cord (the heavy one shown to the left of the device) that connects to the recorder upon which the finished tape is being recorded. The final product is a single tape that includes the mixed sounds (music, sound effects, narration) from the various original sources.

114

About the Author

Robert V. Bullough, Sr., is Associate Professor in the Graduate School of Education, University of Utah. He holds a Ph.D. in Instructional Media and Administration, and a Master's degree in Painting and Sculpture. A practicing artist, he is represented in a number of private and public collections.

His teaching background includes 15 years as teacher and media coordinator (graphics) in the public schools, and 15 years as graphics supervisor and instructor in media at the university level.

Among his publications are two college texts on the production of teaching materials and several articles in such journals as *Educational Technology, Audiovisual Instruction,* and *Industrial Education.*

He currently teaches courses in graphic production, visual perception, visual literacy, and photography.